Studies and documents on cultural policies

In this series:

The serial numbering of titles in this series, the presentation of which has been modified, was
discontinued with the volume *Cultural policy in Italy*

Cultural policy

in Hungary

A survey prepared under the auspices of the
Hungarian National Commission for Unesco

The Unesco Press
Paris 1974

Published by the Unesco Press
7 Place de Fontenoy, 75700 Paris
Printed by Imprimerie des
Presses Universitaires de France, Vendôme

ISBN 92–3–101169–3
French edition: 92–3–201169–7

PN (HUN)

Preface

The purpose of this series is to show how cultural policies are planned and implemented in various Member States.

As cultures differ, so does the approach to them; it is for each Member State to determine its cultural policy and methods according to its own conception of culture, its socio-economic system, political ideology and technical development. However, the methods of cultural policy (like those of general development policy) have certain common problems; these are largely institutional, administrative and financial in nature, and the need has increasingly been stressed for exchanging experiences and information about them. This series, each issue of which follows as far as possible a similar pattern so as to make comparison easier, is mainly concerned with these technical aspects of cultural policy.

In general, the studies deal with the principles and methods of cultural policy, the evaluation of cultural needs, administrative structures and management, planning and financing, the organization of resources, legislation, budgeting, public and private institutions, cultural content in education, cultural autonomy and decentralization, the training of personnel, institutional infrastructures for meeting specific cultural needs, the safeguarding of the cultural heritage, institutions for the dissemination of the arts, international cultural co-operation and other related subjects.

The studies, which cover countries belonging to differing social and economic systems, geographical areas and levels of development, present therefore a wide variety of approaches and methods in cultural policy. Taken as a whole, they can provide guidelines to countries which have yet to establish cultural policies, while all countries, especially those seeking new formulations of such policies, can profit by the experience already gained.

This study was prepared under the auspices of the Hungarian National Commission for Unesco.

The opinions expressed are the authors' and do not necessarily reflect the views of Unesco.

Contents

Introduction

The evolutionary periods and historical values of Hungarian culture were always characteristically linked with movements of social progress, with revolutions and fights for independence. This correlation has deepened contacts with other nations and enabled Hungarian culture to become part of universal culture and directly enrich it through the best of its own national values. Ever since King Stephen I, founder of the Hungarian State, introduced his people ten centuries ago to the then progressive ideology of Christian Europe, the best Hungarian thinkers, poets, writers have, in the spirit of humanism, of the Reformation and of the French Enlightenment, tried creatively to lead the people onwards. In the works of our great national poet Sándor Petőfi, the revolution and the war of independence of 1848 echoed the ideology of the great French Revolution, while the Socialist Revolution of 1919 and the Hungarian Republic of Councils were conceived in the spirit of Marxism.

But the history of Hungarian culture has also carried the imprint of the Turkish occupation of a century and a half, from the mid-sixteenth century to the end of the seventeenth; and of the loss of national independence and prolonged Habsburg rule. Apart from oppression there was the internal weakness of progressive social forces, of belated bourgeois development, of the reactionary, chauvinistic and cultural policy of the former Hungarian ruling classes.

When in 1945 the liberation of Hungary opened up a wide scope for the creative powers of the Hungarian people, we had to face the grave and burdensome consequences of cultural backwardness deriving from belated historical development and from the crimes of the ruling classes. At the same time the road was opened to carry on the best traditions of the Hungarian cultural heritage committed to social progress and to unfold them on a wider scale.

With its laws and measures, as well as with its spirit, the Hungarian Republic of Councils of 1919 definitely committed itself to the progressive

Hungarian and international cultural heritage. During the short months of its existence it tackled dynamically and successfully the revolutionary transformation of the cultural life of a semi-feudal capitalist system. The Hungarian Republic of Councils nationalized the private and Church-owned educational institutions, separated Church and State, introduced the uniform eight-grade popular school, extended and brought secondary and higher education closer to the social requirements. It launched a wide-scale campaign for liquidating illiteracy, issued decrees for creating workers' universities and schools for training skilled workers; by its film, theatre, library, museum and publishing policy it set about making culture public property, publishing the classics of world literature in cheap editions of wide circulation.

After ruthlessly crushing the Republic of Councils the counter-revolutionary system abolished all cultural measures taken by the Republic of Councils, including those representing the implementation of bourgeois-democratic principles and making up for century-old negligence. The principles underlying cultural education were chauvinism, hostility against other peoples, clericalism and unconditional respect for authority. The Churches were given back their ill-equipped schools and preserved their predominance in primary education down to the end of the Second World War. (In 1937–38 the number of State-owned primary schools was 1,287, as against 4,619 denominational schools.) The types of secondary schools were shaped according to the interests of the ruling classes; the universities—from which the progressive-minded scientists and scholars appointed by the Republic of Councils were dismissed—accepted children of workers and peasants up to a limit of 3 to 4 per cent, and not more. The compulsory six grades of primary school were attended only by 50 per cent of the corresponding age group. Popular education was partly entrusted to societies under ecclesiastic guidance and partly made to serve the aims of irredentism, of chauvinism, racism and later of war propaganda under the guise of 'national education'. The cultural organizations, manifestations, concerts and recitals of the working class were persecuted and often banned by the police. The economic oppression of the peasantry led to cultural backwardness. As recently as the year prior to the Second World War there was no electricity in two-thirds of the villages—preventing not only reading but also educational progress through the radio and the cinema. The number of illiterates in the country of 9 million inhabitants exceeded 600,000.

Nevertheless progressive Hungarian scientific and artistic life did produce significant cultural values even in these years, almost invariably against and despite the ruling system and its cultural policy, often aware of subsequent reprisals, so that these values could only reach a relatively narrow layer of society. It was characteristic of the atmosphere of scientific life that the president of the Hungarian Academy of Sciences was Archduke Joseph Habsburg, without any scientific qualification, while many an outstanding scientific personality was compelled to seek scientific and social freedom abroad. The social sciences were canalized towards the narrow interests of the system, and the official views adopted in cultural policy lagged far behind the level of a bourgeois-democratic approach.

The problems of Hungarian history and of Hungarian cultural life could only be solved by a revolutionarily transformed, rejuvenated Hungarian society relying on the Hungarian and international progressive, socialist traditions and experiences. The democratic transformation following the liberation of the country started the liquidation of the harmful cultural heritage of the past; as a result of the socialist transformation in 1948, a socialist cultural revolution unfolded on the social-economic grounds of building socialism. The social ownership of the means of production made it possible to transform the material foundations of life enabling the working classes, the vast masses, to raise their cultural standards. The cultural revolution, conceived in the Leninist sense, that is, aimed at liquidating the cultural monopoly of the former ruling classes, at making cultural values public property and at releasing the cultural creative activity of the working people, is an epoch-making struggle still going on, a struggle in which the Marx-Leninist party of the Hungarian working class has, from the very outset, played a leading role.

The first important cultural political move of the people's democratic State—upon the initiative of the Hungarian Communist Party—was to create the general school in the year of liberation, in 1945. This is a compulsory, eight-grade school, free of charge, relying on a homogeneous curriculum throughout the country, in towns and villages. Thus the people's democratic State not only raised the age of compulsory schooling from 12 to 14 and the standards of primary popular instruction but also opened the road towards the cultural advancement of the working classes and towards a transformation of the Hungarian school system in a democratic spirit. In 1948, one of the first considerable results of the cultural revolution was the nationalization of schools permitting the denominational, corporative and municipal schools to come under a uniform instructional and educational control.

The reform of secondary education turned the earlier eight-grade grammar schools (for the age group 10–18) into four-grade secondary schools (for the age group 14–18), adding to the classical grammar schools many industrial, agricultural and economic technical schools with a four-year training programme. The training of apprentices was replaced by the theoretical and practical training of skilled workers, relying on the eight grades of the general school. Closely linked with the curricular organizational changes were the educational endeavours in a new spirit pervading the atmosphere in schools, gaining ground parallel to the craving of working-class children for knowledge and learning in all types of schools.

Together with the transformation of public education, the reorganization of university and college instruction was also started. In the course of the cultural revolution, highly qualified Marxist and progressive scholars of international reputation came to occupy the university chairs; the widening influence of communist and left-wing youth organizations, the movement of the people's colleges of working-class and peasant origin and educating mainly youth, the growing number of such students shifted the power relations to the benefit of the popular forces. In the early fifties the structure of Hungarian higher education was extended and, besides the universities of arts and sciences, higher education in technical sciences also came close to the best European level by the creation of a university for heavy industry at Miskolc, one for the chemical industries at Veszprém, and by expanding the Budapest Technical University almost twofold.

Within a very short time, the social composition of the students of higher education also underwent a radical change; the share of students of working-class or peasant origin rose from 3–4 per cent in 1938 to 50 per cent in the fifties. For some years these students enjoyed priority in admissions to universities, but this discrimination was abolished in 1962. The stability and efficiency of Hungarian cultural educational policy is evinced by the fact that the proportion of students of working-class or peasant origin in higher education has since remained unchanged. Beside the old intelligentsia, workers and peasants, their sons and daughters have in the past two decades produced a new intelligentsia whose members have occupied various posts in the intellectual life of the country. This is how one of the main objectives of the cultural revolution has materialized.

As a result of the Hungarian socialist educational system, the share—in the population above 15 years of age—of primary-school graduates has risen from 15 to 52 per cent, the share of the general school graduates from 4 to 16 per cent (of those above 18), and the share of graduates from institutions of higher education from 1.6 to 4.3 per cent (of those above 25).

The other great field of the cultural revolution is adult education, including extramural cultural activities. During the first years following the liberation of the country cultural impacts reached much wider layers of the population than in the past. Thousands of courses of lectures were started to liquidate illiteracy; free schools and free universities were opened in towns and villages. The dissemination of culture became an activity under conscious State guidance, the fundamental task of which has ever since been the raising of the cultural standards of the workers and peasants and the encouragement of the development of socialist consciousness with a view to building up a socialist society. A network for the dissemination of culture was developed to cover the whole country; on the strength of the new Museum Act of 1949 the museums occupied their due place among the important cultural and intellectual workshops of the country. An extraordinarily high number of copies of the best works of Hungarian and world literature were published after 1954 under the guidance of the Publishers' Council and Publishers' Board. The rejuvenated Hungarian dramatic and cinematic arts, music reared on Béla Bartók's artistic heritage and in the wake of Zoltán Kodály's educational reform in music teaching, as well as fine arts achieved their deepest ever contact with working people.

In the Hungarian People's Republic there are today more than 3,000 cultural centres, 4,000 youth clubs and almost 200,000 participants in the activities of amateur artistic groups. The 20 million books bought and the 55 million books borrowed annually in libraries, the 7 million visitors to museums a year, the 5 million theatre-goers and the 80 million cinema-goers, the 2.5 million radio listeners and the more than 2 million viewers of television (started in 1956), reveal the extent to which the masses in a Hungary of 10 million inhabitants building socialism have taken possession of culture. Together with the achievements of the educational system, all this has contributed to the high standards of the up-to-date and uniform basic culture of the Hungarian people.

General principles
underlying cultural policy

Through its content and functions, culture is inseparably linked with the society in which it emerges and develops. This is one of the reasons why, in any society, the leading force, the political power, the State, never remains indifferent to culture. In ever-changing forms and on different levels of consciousness, the State has always endeavoured to make culture express the characteristics and promote the objectives of the given society. The general policy and the cultural policy of a State are always co-ordinated.

The society of the Hungarian People's Republic has laid the foundations of socialism and is aware of the task of building it up integrally. In the last analysis its cultural policy is determined by this situation, and by the political tasks deriving from it. Consequently, the general aim of Hungarian cultural policy is to unfold the cultural revolution in the Leninist sense, which is necessarily an integral part, an epochal and permanent task of building up socialism. The evolution of culture is inseparable from the development of socialist economy and society. This is what creates constantly improving objective conditions for solving historically produced contradictions like those between élite and mass culture, between physical and intellectual work; and this is what creates constantly better material and social conditions for the mass assimilation of cultural values, for the harmonious evolution of the many-sided creative powers of the personality. On the other hand, the internal development of culture, its extensive and intensive dissemination at a proper rate and in proper dimensions constitute an all-important condition and stimulation for building socialism, without which neither the immediate nor the long-term economic, social objectives of the Hungarian People's Republic can be implemented.

The notion of the democratization of culture arises in this connexion. The democratization of culture and cultural democracy are related concepts but are not identical. The term 'democratization' implies that intellectual values are the property or privilege of a minority, and democratization means that these values are to be transferred—in a patronizing manner—to

14

the majority who, on the other hand, are uneducated and ignorant. In Hungary this concept has never been adopted by anybody in the past twenty-five years although the main intention for a long time was the transfer of intellectual values. True enough, under certain historical and social conditions, this is the first chapter in cultural democracy, but in Hungary this approach is already a thing of the past. Correctly interpreted cultural democracy expresses the principle that there is no minority and majority in culture, that everybody is part of the public—writers, artists, philosophers alike. Consequently, cultural democracy means that everybody has an equal right to the values of culture, to the old and the new ones, to the classics and to the experimental values, to the easily digestible offerings of art as much as to more condensed mental nutriment. This principle has for long decades been professed and propounded by progressive people, mainly by socialist thinkers. In socialist countries, as in Hungary, a further step has been made in practice: it is the duty of society and of the State to give scope to the cultural right of everybody and to meet cultural demands. This principle was adopted and proclaimed by the world conference on cultural policies in Venice in 1970: 'It is the duty of the governments to shape a clear and comprehensive cultural policy.'

The content of culture, the interpretation of its social functions are influenced and, in the last analysis, determined by historico-social transformations, by the interests of the classes expressing it, even though through several transmissions. The leading power of the Hungarian People's Republic is the working class allied with the other working classes and groups. This is why cultural policy—in keeping with the general objectives of cultural development—makes every effort to ensure that the ideology of the working class, Marx-Leninist ideology, should pervade culture and cultural life as productively as possible.

The makers and activists of Hungarian cultural policy are aware of, and adapt their activity to, the fact that culture—despite its extraordinary complexity—is a homogeneous whole, that its domains—from high-standard literary and artistic creations through production culture down to the behavioural and environmental culture of everyday life—are closely interlinked and intensively interact with one another; that culture, therefore, cannot by any means be reduced to the rational knowledge of the individual sectors, nor does its dissemination boil down simply to 'transmission' and 'assimilation'.

Accordingly, cultural policy in Hungary takes first into consideration the mutual interaction and unity of material and spiritual culture and, relying on the potentialities of socialist society, promotes their uniform and harmonious development. In Hungary culture is considered a manner of living. The distorted ways of life that go with industrial-economic growth in many parts of the world, the phenomena suggesting a diverging development of material welfare and culture are looked upon as incidents that can and should be avoided and overcome. In industrial-economic growth,

15

in the exploitation of the achievements of the scientific and technological revolution, cultural policy sees not only a guarantee of developing the material preconditions of sensible life but also a new possibility of cultural progress, of transforming growing leisure time into productive time.

The totality and unity of culture taken in the above sense, in the last analysis, reflects the many-sidedness of the complex activities of man successfully coping with the forces of nature and society. The epoch-making task of cultural policy in this respect, its historical objective materializing step by step is to render accessible this unity and totality of culture to every individual through the participation of the masses. The unity of culture enables man to achieve a many-sided and harmonious development, personal integrity in the course of building up socialism and communism. This is usually termed the new dimension of culture.

Cultural policy proceeds from the deep and close contacts between cultural values and social progress, regarding socialism, Marx-Leninism and, consequently, socialist culture as an achievement of the development of human culture over thousands of years. Hence the insistence on the integration of the rich progressive national traditions, of the cultural values of the past and of the millennial classical cultural heritage of mankind into Hungarian spiritual, intellectual life. Governed by the internationalism of Marx-Leninism, socialist cultural policy proceeds from the theoretical unity of the national validity and universality of culture, encouraging its evolution. It contributes particularly to the creation and propagation of domestic scientific and artistic values, tackling the substantial, central problems of contemporary Hungarian society and promoting socialist consciousness and morality, thereby ensuring and strongly stimulating the wide-scale domestic dissemination of all progressive, primarily socialist cultural values of the contemporary world. Socialist cultural policy encourages the presentation, translation and publication of contemporary foreign literary and artistic creations which, in a humanist spirit, reflect the aspects of the people of our days and of the contemporary world and contribute on a high artistic level to the understanding of society and of the human mind.

The fundamental endeavours of Hungarian cultural policy are aimed at enabling wider and wider masses to take in and assimilate culture moulded in the spirit of the above principles and thereby to become active participants in, and contributors to, its development. Relying on the general achievements of socialist construction, cultural policy is meant to use all available means to help the development of contacts between culture and the masses, and to ward off all obstacles in the way of this development. Aware of the low level of cultural demands in certain categories and of the uneven distribution of cultural facilities in various regions and social strata, cultural policy regards this state of affairs—however much has been attained—as a transitional and remediable situation, rejecting the duality of 'élite culture' and 'mass culture' (or 'consumers' culture'), the views insisting on their confrontation as a necessity as well as the culturo-political practices based on them.

Since the influencing activity of cultural policy simultaneously extends to, and relies on, the creative intellectuals, on the system of cultural media and on the masses absorbing culture, it concentrates on the integrity of cultural progress. It prompts the creative minds incessantly to look for the possibilities and to evolve the methods by which the masses can be influenced. The entire system of cultural media—educational institutions, book publishers, the press, the mass media, the network of general education (houses of culture, clubs), the apparatus destined to propagate knowledge (museums, libraries), the cultural workshops—are encouraged and inspired to disseminate cultural values as widely as possible, to reduce discrepancies in cultural facilities. It is extremely important to trace demand: to meet the differentiated cultural requirements of the masses and, at the same time, to provoke new demands of rich content. This means that cultural policy based on the growing demands of the masses uses all available material means constantly to improve the subjective conditions of absorbing culture; that is, to arouse the interest of individuals in culture. Consequently it endeavours to raise the general contemporary educational level, the professional knowledge, the artistic culture of the masses. It ensures publicity for the judgements and suggestions of cultural opinion on culture enabling it to exert its influence on the work of the cultural institutions and, in the last analysis, on cultural creative work. This is how the cultural activities and demands of the masses become more organic factors of the totality of the cultural process.

In discharging these functions and implementing these objectives it is necessary to distinguish between the general aims of socialist culture and the cultural life of the Hungarian socialist society. The foundations of socialism have been laid down in Hungary, but the building up of full socialism has not yet been finished and therefore—despite the significant headway made and the leading position attained by Marx-Leninism—the ideological situation of society is still rather contradictory and complex. Therefore the immediate aim of our cultural policy today is not to secure exclusiveness for Marx-Leninist ideology but to strengthen its hegemony, predominance and leading role. It follows that Hungarian cultural policy gives a certain scope and even a certain amount of State support to the creation, the diffusion and the recognition of non-Marxist, non-socialist Hungarian cultural values—books, periodicals, plays, films, paintings, etc.—that are not hostile to socialism.

This principle and its concomitant in practice prevail also internationally. Creations relying on non-Marx-Leninist ideology, humanistic cultural values committed to the people, to labour, to peace, to reason are also given a respectable place in the integrity of Hungarian cultural intellectual life. In addition—especially under the improving conditions of peaceful coexistence—Hungarian cultural policy encourages the establishment and

17

intensification of cultural relations with countries having a different social system, and is ready to exchange experiences promoting the intellectual and material prosperity of the peoples and growing confidence in one another.

At the same time cultural policy ensures, encourages and assists Marxist thinking in all walks of cultural life to confront domestic and foreign humanist values through critical analysis with socialist humanism and to contribute, by criticism and by initiating debates, to a critical assimilation of these values.

As to the freedom of culture, Hungarian cultural policy starts from the principle that a freedom wishing to achieve integrity at the price of refusing to distinguish between value and trash, between cultural and anticultural products is untenable and formal. Relying on this principle it applies administrative measures (prohibition, vetoing) to prevent the circulation of products spreading pornography and sadism and prohibits the publication of domestic or foreign products inciting to racial hatred or war, or directed against socialism and the people.

The structure of Hungarian cultural life, the mechanism of management are based on the co-ordination of central ideological guidance and decentralized execution. Attached to the leading bodies of the Hungarian Socialist Workers' Party is the Cultural Policy Panel, functioning as a consultative body with the participation of many outstanding artists and scholars. From time to time this panel examines and discusses the phenomena, the problems of cultural life, activities in the arts, literature, general education and so on, assessing the achievements and pointing out the short-comings. The statements of the Cultural Policy Panel are important instruments of cultural guidance. The central party and State authorities (the departments of the central committee and the Ministry of Culture) and the attached councils, corporations and collectives put on their agenda and analyse from time to time the state of sciences, arts, education, the dissemination of knowledge and culture or some associated problems, outlining thereby the objectives, the tasks and the methods and means required for their implementation. In compliance with the requirements of the general policy the central party bodies and the Ministry of Culture mould the general principles of cultural policy with due regard to the practical and local experiences and modify the pattern of cultural life, the system of cultural institutions and workshops and the principles of financing in accordance with the emerging new requirements.

The management is a democratic one which means that in all essential questions of cultural life decisions are taken with respect to the opinions of the eminent representatives of the various branches. Organizational proofs of this practice are the various advisory, consultative bodies and collectives attached to management on different levels. This principle and practice constitute important guarantees for eliminating subjectivism and for taking into account the specific features of the given cultural domain.

18

An indispensable concomitant and characteristic trait of the guidance and democratism of cultural life with the use of ideological means is to have intensive debates on the various forums of cultural life, in the creative workshops, in periodicals, on radio, on television and in the press—often accompanied by a very active and vivid participation of the public. The chiefly theoretico-ideological direction of culture is shown also by the fact that these debates are often initiated and always followed with keen interest by the makers of cultural policy which from time to time invests the lessons drawn with cultural-political validity.

Associated with this is the important task of management to ensure and promote the democratism of cultural public life with its own means. Cultural management consistently fights against the appearance of any kind of protocol-like approach, of clique or group hegemony, against their acquiring monopolistic positions. Cultural life certainly knows and recognizes authorities, but this must not involve the repression of limitation of other opinions. Authority achieved or functions performed in cultural life must not result in creating or securing exclusiveness for an artistic trend, for a scientific school or—in the worst case—for faction or group interests. Among other things it is the duty of management to see to it that no leaders of any institution should get into a position in which they can defeat their adversaries in the debate by administrative measures.

The system of material incentives plays a substantial part in cultural management. The esteem of the people's State for culture is eloquently shown by the fact that the principal source for financing culture is not profit but State and social funds that increase with the growth of the national income.

The theoretico-ideological guidance and the system of material incentives and regulators operated in the spirit of this guidance is, as a matter of course, complemented by the administrative activity of the State and the social apparatus of cultural life.

Organization of cultural administration

Higher management

The highest body of special administration for culture, general and public education is the Ministry of Culture, headed by the minister elected by parliament as a member of the government.

The administration of the relations between State and Church, the State supervision of denominational schools have, since 1951, been the task of a separate authority, the State Office for Church Affairs, which is headed by the president, ranking as an under-secretary of State.

The highest authority charged with matters of the press is the Council of Ministers' Information Office, which is headed by a president ranking as an under-secretary of State.

The Hungarian Radio and Television are directly subordinated to the Council of Ministers and are headed by a president.

The international cultural affairs of the Hungarian People's Republic are taken care of by the Institute for Cultural Relations, which is headed by a president.

The Minister of Culture takes part in the shaping of the cultural policy of the government, contributes to co-ordinating cultural policy and economic policy, formulates the tasks of the country's cultural policy and provides for a co-ordinated management and control of the sectoral specialized work by which these tasks are implemented.

MINISTRY OF CULTURE

The competence of the Ministry of Culture extends to the following:

Culture.[1] Literature (literary periodicals; the Fund for Literature within the Art Fund of the Hungarian People's Republic; Federation of Hungarian Writers).

---

1. 'Arts' in domestic terminology.

Book publishing and selling (book-publishing and bookselling enterprises; Union of Publishers; copyright).

Theatre, music and dancing (theatrical and musical institutions; periodicals; production and distribution of records; the Fund for Music within the Art Fund of the Hungarian People's Republic; Association of Hungarian Dramatic Artists; Association of Hungarian Musical Artists; Association of Hungarian Dance Artists; Institute for Theatre Science).

Film production and distribution, national network of cinemas (institutions, enterprises; periodicals; Association of Hungarian Film and Television Artists; Institute for Film Science).

Fine arts and applied arts (periodicals; the Fund for Fine Arts and its enterprises within the Art Fund; Association of Hungarian Artists, Painters and Sculptors).

Instruction in arts (institutions of primary, secondary and higher education).

General education. Cultural homes and similar institutions; extramural cultural movements; dissemination of knowledge; periodicals; Institute for Culture.

Scientific, specialized and public libraries; periodicals; National Technical Library and Documentation Centre.

Museums and archives; periodicals; Central Board for Museums.

Public education. Primary, secondary and higher education; protection of children and youth; National Pedagogical Institute; Pedagogical Research Centre for Higher Education; National Centre for Instruction Technology; National Pedagogical Library and Museum; Enterprise for Producing and Distributing Educational Appliances.

The various branches enumerated above are taken care of by departments and sections of the ministry.

The direct superior authorities of the cultural institutions coming under the ministry are usually the councils of the capital, the towns and districts (except for institutes of higher education, some institutions for the protection of children and some theatres of national importance). The ministry co-operates closely with the heads and cultural sections of these councils.

The minister operates through decrees and instructions. He supports specialized work and the councils through guidelines, and an information system on cultural matters. The work of the ministry, its departments, scientific institutes and specialized periodicals is analysed and assessed; debates and criticisms are also used to provide guidance.

Direct control is exerted partly (to a lesser extent) by experts invited by the ministry, and partly (to a larger extent) by workshops, the leading corporations and the cultural sections of the councils. The ministry may order these councils to report to him on all or part of their activities.

The workshops are mainly teams of artists from the official, institutional

21

apparatus that promotes the development of arts (e.g. book publishing enterprises, editorial boards of periodicals, theatres, film studios, orchestras and so on). They enjoy independence in the planning and execution of their own work, and in utilizing the funds made available to them. Their managers carry a one-man responsibility for the activities of the workshop but rely on advisory bodies in preparing their decisions and in performing their work. The extensive independence of the workshops guarantees the practical implementation of the general principles, directly adapted to the specific features of the special domains including—in the absence of censorship—decisions on publishing. The superior authorities (the ministry and the councils) use directives and economic regulators in exercising control over their work and may order them to render account of their activities.

Attached to the ministry are several co-ordinating and advisory bodies, operating upon the request of the minister, e.g. Publishers' Council, Dramatic Art Council, Musical Art Council, Dance Art Council, Cinematographic Art Council, Fine Arts Council, Applied Arts Council, Library Council. The following operate on the request of the government, partly as bodies responsible to it: National Council for Public Culture; National Council for Youth Policy and Education.

Council management

The regional and local autonomous and administrative bodies—the capital, town and village councils—play an important part in implementing cultural policy. In the management of cultural affairs the councils are autonomous within their territory; they are responsible for their activities to the higher councils and, to a large extent, to parliament. Depending on the size of their territory, a cultural section, group or official assists them in their work, and in putting their decisions into practice.

The territorial bodies of State administration are the county councils and the council of the capital. On their territories they are responsible for the enforcement of the central cultural and political policies, and determine the main principles governing the activity of the local councils in cultural matters affecting the county or capital.

The councils are entitled to establish cultural institutions (e.g. libraries, centres of culture, museums, archives, secondary schools) to meet the demands of the entire territory or of several towns, villages or districts.

The local bodies of State administration are the councils of county towns, other towns, the various districts of the capital, the large villages and of villages.

Institutions meeting the fundamental cultural demands of the population are created and maintained by the local councils (for instance, libraries, houses of culture, theatres, professional choirs and orchestras, folk-dance and ballet ensembles, institutions of primary education and, in some cases, even secondary schools).

The work of institutions entrusted to take care of certain branches of cultural activities is co-ordinated by the local councils. The councils co-operate with the trade unions, with the Patriotic People's Front and other large organizations. They may exercise control over non-council bodies, checking whether they observe the legal rules adopted in cultural matters in the interest of the workers and may ask these to report on their activities. Jointly with the non-council bodies they are entitled to establish and operate cultural institutions.

Cultural activities of social organizations

Several social organizations help to provide certain categories of adult workers and youth with cultural facilities and ensure their active participation in cultural life:

The National Council of Trade Unions (SZOT) and the trade unions (for the iron workers, teachers, etc.) operate a separate network of cultural homes and libraries, as an outstanding feature in their cultural activities.

The National Council of Production Co-operatives (TOT) and the co-operative centres (the National Federation of Co-operatives, the National Federation of Industrial Co-operatives, the National Organization of Artisans).

The Communist Youth Federation (KISZ) and the Pioneers' National Federation.

The Society for the Dissemination of Scientific Knowledge (TIT).

Financing culture

Cultural activities (preservation of cultural heritage, the creation of new values, dissemination of culture in the widest possible sense) are materially supported by the socialist State. Accordingly, the cultural institutions and enterprises (museums, public libraries, homes of culture, theatres, book publishers, film studios, etc.) are maintained by the State, by the councils or the trade unions which ensure most of the personal, material and objective conditions necessary for their operation. The material support is provided mainly through grants from the central budget, development funds of the councils, credits and development funds of the enterprises.

The main reason why material assistance granted to cultural activities is indispensable is that the price level of cultural products and services (books, theatre and cinema tickets, etc.) is—in keeping with the principles outlined above underlying the cultural policy of the socialist State—so low that the income of cultural institutions and enterprises does not cover the prime costs. Thus, for instance, the price of a theatre ticket (as bought by the public) on an average covers only one-third of the 'theatre prime cost' calculated for one theatre ticket, while the rest is paid from a State grant. State assistance amounts by and large to the same or similar proportions in the prices of other cultural activities and services. This system of assistance enables the creative workshops (theatres, film studios, book publishers) to serve cultural interests under relatively favourable material conditions determined by the financial situation of the country, and makes the creations of culture accessible to all members of society.

Cultural and artistic activities of outstanding value and importance for the socialist society are thus in a privileged position when subsidies are distributed. For instance, museums, public libraries and cultural homes are open to the public for a negligible entrance fee. The works of the classics of Hungarian and world literature can in general be bought for a price substantially lower than, for instance, thrillers or novels of adventure meant to satisfy demands for entertainment.

Further financial allowances are meant to promote the dissemination of cultural and artistic creations and to arouse the interest of youth and of the workers. Season tickets for youth at half price for concerts encourage the development of musical culture of the younger generation. The series of performances at reduced prices for youth have considerably expanded the numbers of young theatre-goers.

The system of subsidizing cultural activities has successfully contributed to the development of cultural life and to the dissemination of culture in Hungarian society.

General education[1]

The socialist social order established in Hungary after the liberation of the country could not rest content with the social education inherited from the past, that is, among other things, with the fact that the majority of the working class possessed the barest minimum of knowledge necessary for performing labour. Parallel to the political transformation, a cultural revolution was started—and is still going on—which is destined to raise the cultural level of the entire society, to concentrate on a culture imbued with the ideas of Marx-Leninism and with progressive ideals, on socialist culture encompassing all valuable creations of the history of mankind built on this historical tradition.

General education has an important part to play in this social and cultural revolution since such an epoch-making change cannot be achieved merely through public education: all means, forms and institutions of extra-mural education must be made use of in a conscious and planned manner.

The cultural requirements of socialism make it indispensable for the leading class of the society, the working class and the allied peasantry to achieve an educational level enabling it—as a class—to exercise power and to create a really humanist social order. To this end the first step was the schooling of workers and peasants who had come to occupy leading posts in public and economic life, that is, the creation of possibilities for them to acquire the education they needed. The same end was pursued by political and ideological instruction embracing most of the fundamental working classes, the rapid development of instructional and educational institutions and by widely opening the possibilities of access to education and culture.

Following from the nature of the new society, all categories of workers must naturally acquire all the knowledge through which economic, municipal and social democracy acquires a more and more lively content. Socialism requires all citizens to achieve a well-founded historical, social,

1. Covering the activities of houses of culture, clubs, libraries, museums and so on.

legal and economic education and a permanent flexibility for adapting themselves to rapid development.

It is part and parcel of socialism to fight for the full liberation of man, for the self-assertion of the collective core of his creative personality. This, however, can only be achieved if people are given the chance of evolving their own personalities, of acquiring the learning and education necessary for understanding scientific creations and for assimilating artistic values.

The rapid rate of development of material production also makes it necessary to widen the educational scope of schooling and of extramural education, essentially to raise the standards of scientific and vocational instruction.

After the victory of the socialist revolution tremendous changes were wrought in the structure of our society. Owing to rapid industrial development, the working class has grown threefold and the number of intellectual workers has also increased considerably whereas—with the creation of large socialist agricultural enterprises and with the industrialization of agriculture—the peasantry, which used to make up the majority of society, has diminished to one-quarter of the population. This restratification has had its impact on general education, too.

The sudden boosting of the number of workers meant that the majority of them had acquired their knowledge and professional skills in their earlier capacity as peasants or smallholders. Their adaptation has had to be and still has to be encouraged by means of schooling and general education. Their world outlook, social endeavours and individual way of life are still closely linked with the traditions, with the morals inherited from their earlier living conditions. In addition to the educative effect of the new way of life, it is the duty of general education to lead these new groups—by moulding their minds and education—to recognize, accept and actively support the objectives of collective society.

The social and economic structure, the rapid technical development of the relatively young, large socialist enterprises established in agriculture require emotional, conscious and educational accommodation also from the peasantry. To encourage this adaptation with various means and in diverse forms is another task of general education.

Economic development, which is becoming more and more intensive, also influences the tasks of general education. This is because the pool upon which industry and services can rely in order to meet their new manpower demands is becoming more and more restricted, and also because the reconstruction of certain industries, the mechanization of processes requiring heavy physical work, automation and the use of computers require more and more specialized training and retraining which necessarily goes hand in hand with the necessity of further diffusing scientific knowledge and artistic values.

Owing to socio-economic development the standard of living of the country's population has risen substantially, especially in the last decade.

This permits changes and further development in the traditional way of life of the population on a social scale. The improvement of economic facilities and the reduction of working time have created opportunities for sports and cultural activities, for a reasonable utilization of the creative energies of people. This change in the way of life is, however, no spontaneous process. Many examples throughout the world prove that better material circumstances may create opportunities for a substantial part of the society to increase their own burden, to contract debts and to submit personal desires to imaginary or real questions of prestige. By increasing the role of general education we wish to avoid getting into this impasse of development.

The developments achieved in social education, the considerable rise in the level of qualifications, the wide-scale diffusion of the means of mass communication, the rapid spread of television in particular, the high attendance in cultural institutions testify to an unprecedented demand for cultural alimentation as well as to the fact that these demands are to be satisfied on a higher level than before. Parallel to the rise of the cultural level and to the improvement of material and technical conditions the work and co-operation of cultural institutions must also be improved in order to meet social and individual requirements.

Two networks of general education have so far developed in parallel in Hungary: the residential network of libraries, clubs, cultural homes; and the enterprise network of these institutions. The former are sustained by the local councils, the latter by the trade unions. In the future this duality will systematically be developed further. In the villages where the residential community and the community of the place of work are not separated, only one system, the council network, will be necessary, yet the advantages of the duality will be made use of by combining the convenience of the closeness of the homes with the cohesive force of the communities at the places of work. The role of the workers' and youth organizations, of the trade unions and of the Communist Youth Federation in the organization of general education will be enhanced.

Unlike the other major factor of education—the school—which is partly compulsory and has more strictly organized and institutionalized forms, general education is based on voluntary participation. The driving force of such forms is the moral power of communities evolving in work, in learning, in youth organizations giving permanent stimuli for exploiting the possibilities created institutionally. Such a collective form is the movement of socialist brigades encompassing all producing enterprises in Hungary. The idea is that the participants of the movement—by voluntarily undertaking various tasks—should learn to live, to work and to educate themselves in a socialist manner. In other words, beyond the actual duties connected with work, the movement wishes to develop personality and to create a rich collective life.

Pedagogical and sociological experiences eloquently prove that the most valuable, the most successful mode of education is any form requiring practical work: one of the firmest foundations of assessing high artistic values and of assimilating scientific achievements is activity of an artistic or scientific character pointing in some definite direction. Singing and acting, puppetry and do-it-yourself hobbies, interest in local history and folklore or any other similar kind of activity create a sound basis for artistic and scientific receptivity. Beginning from spontaneous singing, collective activity may assume a wide variety of forms and culminate in artistic and scientific creation. But beyond the active understanding and involved personality, so important for the education of socialist man, our reason for trying to develop this educational form is that the active assimilation of culture usually requires a collective framework. Beside communities shaped by work, cultural communities are also suitable for training members of a collective society. This active and collective form of cultural education corroborates and also implies a dynamic character in general education.

Various forms of entertainment are also considered to come under the heading of general education. Entertainment that provides recreation and rest is a natural desire but it should be satisfied in a manner justifying and stimulating interest in deep intellectual values and their assimilation. Forms of entertainment which do not necessarily have an artistic value are not necessarily opposed to real art. There is, however, a definite endeavour to reduce, in fact, to fight off, trash that diverts taste from real art.

Relying on our achievements we wish to evolve a consistent general educational attitude in scientific and artistic life, in the activities of scientific and artistic institutions, which are meant to formulate a long-term educational programme in a conscious manner to govern their further activities. The main tasks under this programme consist of satisfying the demands of the art-lovers on a higher level than before and to extend the sphere of the competent public by arousing the interest of the large masses in arts and sciences. An important part of this work is to acquaint the public with the new idioms of art.

Owing to the growth of social demands, general education has come into the focus of social interest. General education is understood to mean lifelong education of the members of the society, including extramural and self-educational, entertaining, informative and recreational activities for acquiring higher forms of knowledge and making better use of leisure.

General education materializes in a constantly changing, multi-sectored (State, social and place of work) and multi-level practice on the basis of uniform principles of cultural policy, in compliance with local conditions and specific circumstances under the guidance of cultural State authorities.

In close interaction with the education of consciousness, ethical and emotional education is the task of active cultural communities, which thereby help to achieve our social objectives. General education is part and parcel of the cultural revolutionary process which induces Hungarian citizens to realize and shoulder the tasks deriving from the social objectives and whose chief driving force is at the same time the cultural, the public activity of the masses.

State direction of general education

The highest managerial State authority in general of adult education is the Ministry of Culture. Its responsibility for general education extends to the general educational activities of all State and social organizations. The major tasks are:

To formulate development conceptions and proposals for the totality and individual sectors of general education.

To assess implementation from the angle of special vocational education.

To secure the conditions and means necessary for the implementation of policy within national economic planning.

To regulate the proper operation of institutions.

To maintain institutions of national importance (national library, museums, institutes of culture, etc.).

Attached to sections and departments taking care of various branches of general education are advisory bodies, consisting of the appropriate experts and representatives of the maintaining authorities (e.g. the National Council for Libraries and Documentation, the National Council for Museums, the National Council for Cultural Homes).

More than one State authority is concerned with general education. In addition to such central State institutions as, for instance, Hungarian Radio and Television (see below), general educational work is performed and controlled, e.g. by the Ministry of Agriculture and Food (courses in agricultural training), the Ministry for Public Health (health education), the Ministry for Building and Urban Development (protection and utilization of monuments), and so on.

The role of the centres of social organizations and of organizations for the protection of the workers' interests (e.g. the National Council of Trade Unions, the Hungarian Communist Youth Federation, the National Federation of Co-operatives, the National Council of Production Co-operatives) in the central management of general education has also gained in significance. Their main task is to guide activities performed by themselves and in the institutions maintained by them, but they also take part in moulding the concepts of the country's general educational policy.

The co-ordination of the work of organizations engaged in, and exercising control over, general education is the task of the National Council for General Education. Taking part in its work are the heads of State authorities (ministries) and social organizations concerned with general education, eminent artists and scientists, as well as specialists working in various types of major institutions of general education.

The general education policy of the State is put into practice by the local authorities, the councils (see above). Their major tasks are:

With the help of social bodies to formulate the general education plan for the territory in question and to co-ordinate the resources and forces for implementation.

To maintain the majority of institutions of general education (libraries, cultural homes, museums, etc.).

To exercise professional control over the general education activities of any organization within the given territory.

These duties are performed in fact by the councils. The local (town and village) councils are responsible for the local institutions. The duties of the councils of territorial administration (county councils) include the transmission of central general education policy, its application to local conditions, and guidance to the lower councils. They maintain the regional institutions of general education (county libraries, museums, etc.).

The operational conditions of the institutions of general education are secured and financed from various sources. Part of the share in the State budget allocated for this purpose appears in the budget of the Ministry of Culture earmarked for central objectives (maintenance of central institutions, support to cultural enterprises, etc.), the other part goes to the county councils within their budget (and is forwarded to the town and village councils). These sums as well as a share of their own incomes assigned for the purpose are used for maintaining institutions of general education, sometimes all operational costs (e.g. in the case of museums), sometimes only a part of them (e.g. in the case of cultural houses).

Enterprises and co-operatives may use part of their incomes for forming tax-free cultural funds which are then utilized by the community concerned. They may either maintain cultural institutions of their own or operate joint undertakings with the councils. They may also use their cultural funds for raising the cultural standards of their own workers (for buying theatre tickets, for excursions, etc.).

The social organizations may use their discretion to decide what part of the membership fees will be assigned to purposes of general education.

In recent years, the creation of institutions of general education has been more and more frequently governed by the co-ordinated utilization of different (State, enterprise, co-operative) resources. Plans for developing networks of institutions are drawn up by the councils, but for their implementation they try to engage also the energies of the local economic and social agencies.

Institutions of general education

HOUSES OF CULTURE

The name 'cultural home' is a comprehensive term for several subdivisions of a type of general education institution discharging a wide diversity of functions. The most important are as follows:

To impart content and form to the social communal life of the given place of work or settlement; to create conditions for common cultural activities and entertainment; this presumes and necessitates a club-like operation.

To provide facilities for people to satisfy their creative desires (amateur scientific and artistic activities).

To provide an environment where people can become acquainted with scientific and artistic activities, particularly in places which have no theatre, exhibition or concert hall.

To take a share—especially in the case of major institutions—in the tasks of adult education.

For the establishment of institutions of this type—perhaps with tasks not as differentiated as these—a veritable social movement was launched in 1949, especially in villages and factories. State resources, local funds and a considerable amount of social work done by the population helped their establishment. In minor forms all extramural cultural facilities were provided by these institutions. The rapid development often resulted in stop-gap arrangements, sometimes only in the form of a great hall. The flexibility, the elasticity of this type of institution, has been proved by the fact that it has always adapted itself to the circumstances, to changing requirements over a quarter of a century.

Changes in requirements have produced the following types—in several stages as from 1965.

The cultural centre is the institution of large villages, towns, big factories; there were 173 of them in 1972. They meet almost every requirement of the system, operating studios, free universities, academies, clubs and amateur groups. Those built recently are real cultural centres, functioning as theatres, cinemas, concert halls, etc., in towns with 30,000 to 40,000 inhabitants.

The cultural houses (1,268 in 1972) are institutions for villages and minor towns with populations between 1,500 and 12,000, as well as for small factories. Here the requirements mentioned in the previous item are met to a lesser extent (fewer groups, smaller halls, etc.) and in co-operation with other institutions.

The club libraries (1,099 in 1972) are found in villages with populations of less than 1,500, and in small factories. They rely mainly on books and television and are at the same time the centres of local communal life.

In addition to those listed above there are a few hundred circles and clubs, but the process outlined has not come to an end, and the creation of various types of institution goes on.

A settlement may house more than one of these institutions, for they are complementary to one another. In a large town, for instance, cultural houses and club libraries—in suburbs or newly settled parts—may be a useful addition to the cultural centre.

The cultural homes are administered by an elected management in compliance with the requirements of the communities supporting them, which have to approve the programmes and the statutes. The implementation is the task of the professionals—specialized employees and technical experts.

31

The significance of the cultural homes can be understood by observing the high number of visitors annually—50 million. The following are their dominant features:

Centred on communal interests, the clubs are organized either by categories (youth, women, the old) or interests (agricultural, technical, do-it-yourself clubs, etc.); their number was 4,378 in 1972, including 2,713 youth clubs.

Amateur ensembles have offered facilities for about 175,000 people to acquaint themselves with or take an active part in various creative activities.

The 6,252 professional circles have allowed over 100,000 people to engage in natural and technical sciences on an amateur level (garden-lovers, modellers, hobby fans, collectors of various kinds of items, enthusiasts of homeland studies, etc.).

They are important bases of adult education and of disseminating knowledge, as shown by the following data for 1972: 1,873 language courses, 4,298 public utility courses (embroidering, tailoring, sewing), 2,061 academies, 151 free universities, and 4,652 courses preparing for school examinations or offering other kinds of adult education. Less formal modes of acquiring knowledge were represented by 41,381 other items, e.g. exhibitions, excursions, film projections, intellectual contests. In addition to all this 100,557 lectures popularizing sciences were delivered in cultural homes to audiences amounting to 4.4 million.

Programmes (evenings with entertainment, dances, club gatherings, projections of feature films) were attended by 6.9 million people in 1972—an attendance that is now diminishing under the impact of television.

Cultural homes operate over 2,000 libraries and as many cinemas. The number of cultural homes in 1972 was 2,825 (2,229 maintained by councils, 453 by trade unions and 143 by other organizations). The majority of institutions maintained by factories are used also by the local population.

Some 50 to 55 per cent of the operational expenses (including the wages of the employees, heating, electricity) is covered from the budget, and the rest from receipts—payments for renting the premises or from entertainments (dances, shows with professional artists). Educational and amateur artistic or scientific activities are free; for courses and club gatherings there is usually a nominal membership fee.

Professional and operational guidance on a national scale is provided by the Institute for Culture which records and analyses experiences, and provides training and further training for the leaders of artistic ensembles and professional circles. A particularly important task of the county cultural centres is to advise and assist minor cultural homes.

The central periodical devoted to the totality of general education, including the cultural homes, is the monthly *Népmüvelés*.

The leaders and professional employees of cultural homes are trained in

Arts course in Turkeve, a provincial town.
[*Photo: MTI, Ferenc Bereth*]

Gothic hall of knights in the reconstructed Buda Castle. [*Photo: MTI, Sándor Mezó*]

Reading-room at a Budapest secondary school. [*Photo: MTI, Endre Friedmann*]

Student hostel of the Agricultural University of Debrecen.
[*Photo: MTI, Pal Laszló Balogh*]

School bus transporting children of scattered rural settlements
to a central district school.
[*Photo: MTI, Vera Kiss*]

New schools in a new district of Budapest.
[*Photo: MTI, Imre Benkő*]

Language laboratory at a provincial secondary school.
[*Photo: MTI, Károly Gottvald*]

Library of the Scientific Collection of the Reformed Church District, Sárospatak.
[*Photo: Ferenc Tulok*]

Examination performance at the College of Drama and Film.
[*Photo: MTI, Eva Keleti*]

universities (five years) and in college-like institutions (three years). A considerable number of teachers obtain basic training in the course of their ordinary studies. A large part of those people who do general education work parallel to working in some other occupation may obtain supplementary training in teachers' courses.

LIBRARIES

One of the major cultural achievements of the past quarter of a century is the establishment of a network of libraries which provide general access to books and periodicals. They bring literature into the smallest town (through council-sponsored libraries) and to the places of work (through trade-union sponsored libraries in factories, enterprises and workers' hostels). These libraries are open to all ages, social strata and groups, with practically all services free of charge. Their significance is shown by the fact that close to one-quarter (2.27 million) of the population are regular users, and the annual number of items borrowed for reading is 58 million, out of the total stock numbering over 28 million volumes.

In addition to offering literature and entertainment, the libraries try to meet demands for self-instruction and information, either from their own stocks (libraries in county centres and in major towns) or from scientific and special libraries which are to be found all over the country.

A uniform library system was created by Law-Decree 5/1956 of the Presidential Council of the People's Republic, which also incorporated the formerly isolated libraries into networks. Beside the library networks of the twenty councils (nineteen county councils and one metropolitan council) and those of the various trade unions, other networks comprise the libraries of the individual national-economic branches and for important scientific subjects. The methodological guidance of close to two thousand scientific and special libraries is taken care of by the national libraries which also provide up-to-date information services.

Among the libraries of educational institutions those in general and secondary schools acquire added importance by the updating of public education. As well as meeting the demands of students and teachers, the university and college libraries take an active part in providing information for research and development.

The leading institution is the National Széchenyi Library, founded in 1802. The National Library is responsible for collecting and preserving copies of all domestic book production, literature published abroad in the Hungarian language or relating to Hungary, and for compiling national bibliographies of books and periodicals issued in Hungary. Besides other central services, it takes care of the international exchange of publications, of distributing copyright copies, etc. Part of the National Library is the Centre for Library Science and Methodology, a central methodological and research agency.

33

Librarians are trained in institutions created since 1945. The Eötvös Lóránd University of Arts and Sciences, Budapest, has a department which awards qualifications in higher education to librarians (coupled with other subjects like Hungarian literature, foreign languages, natural sciences, history, etc.). Special courses and some colleges offer secondary qualifications. Since the liberation some 2,000 librarians have acquired qualifications in higher education, and about 4,000 have medium-level qualifications.

The Association of Hungarian Librarians (a member of the International Federation of Library Associations) has about 1,500 members. Most important of the various periodicals devoted to librarianship are *Könyvtáros*, *Könyvtári Figyelő* and *Magyar Könyvszemle*. The semi-annual abstracting journal *Magyar Könyvtártudományi és Informatikai Irodalom* is published in English (*Hungarian Literature on Library Science and Informatics*) and in Russian.

MUSEUMS

The museums and other public collections constitute a homogeneous network operating on identical principles. The protection of monuments and other items is regulated by Law-Decree 9/1963 of the Presidential Council of the People's Republic and by the decrees of the Minister of Culture.

On the strength of the above decree the institutions of this kind are divided into two large categories:

1. Museums, that is, collections whose operation covers collection, processing and display. Belonging to this category are the national museums, other museums of national scope, county, regional and local museums.
2. Public collections, including memorial sites (memorial museums, memorial houses), collections of local interest, special collections of factories and other institutions.

The museum collections embrace historic items which illustrate the economic, social and cultural development of a given area—a territorial unit. It is characteristic of the Hungarian museums that most of them derive from mixed collections and therefore their collecting activity—mainly in the provinces—operates in many directions. The other main type of museum is meant to collect the totality of historic items relating to a given domain (fine arts, literature, industry) and thus includes special museums.

The co-ordination and the highest superintendence of the work of museums and public collections are taken care of by the Minister of Culture. Directly subordinate to the Museum Department is the Central Board for Museums, responsible for organizing permanent museum exhibitions, the training and further training of restorers, the operation of the restorers' central laboratory, research, taking care of museum investments, preparing and marketing replicas of works of art, organizing publicity.

Museologists are trained in university faculties of arts (five-year course).

34

Museums can be run by the Ministry of Culture, by other ministries and by the councils—the metropolitan council in the capital and the county councils in the provinces.

Museum-type establishments within one county come under a county museum organization under the direct supervision of the county council.

In planning the scientific activity of museums the Ministry of Culture co-operates with the Hungarian Academy of Sciences.

At present there are 189 museums and public collections in Hungary; 39 in Budapest and 150 elsewhere. The growth of the network and the recognition of their importance can be judged from the fact that more museums have been created since 1945 than during the preceding century and a half. In 1938 there were altogether six nation-wide museums: the Hungarian National Museum; the Museum of Natural Sciences; the Museum of Fine Arts; the Museum of Applied Arts; the Agricultural Museum; and the Ethnographical Museum.

The number of collections has likewise increased. Not to speak of the diversity of the objects kept in museums it is worth noting that the number of valuable objects registered in one way or another runs beyond the 2 million mark (over five times the pre-1945 figure).

The most relevant factor for assessing the general education role of museums is the quantitative and qualitative growth of visiting. Permanent and occasional exhibitions using contemporary didactic methods (505 in 1955, 1,009 in 1965, 1,406 in 1972), guided tours, lectures, literary evenings, intellectual competitions and youth competitions attract a growing number of visitors from year to year from among schoolchildren, students, workers in factories and in co-operatives. The number of visitors rose from 791,000 in 1938 and 672,000 in 1949 to 4,460,000 in 1961 and to 7,881,000 in 1972. Increasing attendance and widening educational activities are stimulated by the Month of Museums and Monuments held in Hungary each year in October and by free admission (as from April 1973) to all schoolchildren and students—from the general schools up to the universities—every day of the week, and to the adult population every Saturday.

Protection of monuments

The protection of monuments, which has existed for a century in Hungary, comes under the Ministry of Building and Urban Development, but the cultural administration takes care of the employment of the aesthetic and historical values of relics and monuments for the purposes of general education.

Protection involves safeguarding characteristic and irreplaceable monuments and their surroundings, historical sites, and using them in a manner worthy of their historical and artistic value and character for cultural and tourist purposes.

According to the National Board for Monument Protection (the administrative authority which also supervises relevant research, architectural design and execution) Hungary's 8,251 monuments include 1,859 actually classified as monuments, 5,351 which are 'monument-like', and 1,041 'townscape sites'. Special protection is extended to 13 city centres particularly rich in monuments and historic buildings; and 200 monuments enjoy environmental protection. Protection is co-ordinated with plans of contemporary construction.

Most museums are housed in restored monuments, which thus give worthy surroundings while ensuring the permanent protection and public utilization of the monuments.

Nature conservation

Natural objects are preserved and maintained on scientific or artistic grounds under a law-decree of 1961. They include geological configurations (hills, caves, etc.), waters, plants, plant communities, some wild animals, natural areas and regions. The character of a protected district must not be changed in any manner.

The National Office for Nature Conservation is aided by a council consisting of representatives of the higher authorities, educational institutions, cultural, scientific and other organizations and by the specialized bodies of county administration and by their committees.

Nature conservation is closely linked with educational and cultural objectives. The provision of information about the countryside and the historical past of the homeland, the love of nature, the promotion of tourism are considered part of the work of educational institutions and of general education.

Archives

The archives in Hungary are scientific institutions for receiving, preserving and processing written documents of historical value, but they also have administrative and educational functions.

Part of the country's seventy archive offices are general, part are special. There are two national archives used by the Hungarian National Archives for documents prior to 1945; the New Hungarian Central Archives deal with those dated after 1945. The twenty-one regional general archives receive material from the capital and the counties. There are forty-seven specialized archives—five secular and forty-two ecclesiastic.

The National Archives are superintended by the Minister of Culture; county and metropolitan archives by the councils concerned; while the relevant State, social or ecclesiastic organizations are directly responsible for the special archives.

The technical supervision of county and special archives is the task of the Board for Archives and the Ministry of Culture.

Archives are utilized in general education in the following ways:

They provide material for research in local history; they process such material, compile chronicles, formulate guidelines, analyse problems of local history, and produce studies and source publications, texts of local interest, and encyclopaedias of local history.

They inform visitors about the materials held, arrange lectures in history for school children and organize special courses which are open to the public.

They regularly provide the information media with historical documents of interest for the public.

They organize exhibitions of valuable documents and illustrate the past of a geographical or administrative area, an event of national or local importance or the work of famous men.

The educational activity of archives has proved most successful in places where it is planned in co-operation with libraries and museums.

Archive staff train in a five-year course at the Faculty of Arts in the Eötvös Lóránd University, Budapest.

Educational activities of social institutions

The Society for the Dissemination of Scientific Knowledge (TIT) was established in 1841. Its members are intellectuals who consider the spreading of scientific knowledge as a social vocation. The society plans, implements, and analyses the dissemination of knowledge and the complex processes by which it is done, and tries to enlist as many intellectuals as possible in the propagation of science, and the raising of the cultural standards of society.

The society tries to make up for lacunae in general culture and to promote general and specialized knowledge. It has various educational programmes, and co-operates with other cultural and educational institutions, with factories and enterprises requiring educational services, and issues popular and scientific periodicals and publications.

The society publishes specialized periodicals (*Valóság, Élat és Tudómany, Buvár, Természet Világa* and others).

It is organized in units or sections according to disciplines or administrative areas, under the guidance of a democratically elected presidium. It operates throughout Hungary and has 20,000 lecturers in twenty-four disciplines, e.g. philosophy, literature, Hungarian and foreign languages, economics, arts, international policy, educational theory, biology, astronomy, space research, medical science, agricultural sciences, technical sciences. It arranged 109,000 lectures in 1972 for audiences running to 4.6 million.

MAJOR FORMS USED IN DISSEMINATING
SCIENTIFIC KNOWLEDGE

Ten per cent of all educational lectures consist of individual lectures whose purpose is to inform and provoke interest; 33 per cent of the lectures consist of series devoted to a particular discipline. Some complex series survey a complete range of problems.

The character of academies is determined by the needs of their students. Series involving at least eight lectures a year may continue over years for the same audiences. Workers' and co-operative (agricultural) academies are mostly organized in the place of work, to develop and update general and vocational education by providing relevant knowledge about the social and natural sciences and by imparting specialized vocational information. Youth academies are usually devoted to the specific problems of various categories of youth (students, young workers, peasants), and account for 35 per cent of the educational lectures.

The free universities offer series of advanced lectures on aspects and problems of a particular discipline or art; 26,000 people studied in 279 sections in 1972; this accounted for 10 per cent of lectures.

The summer universities provide higher training for Hungarian and foreign students attending lectures by the best specialists, as well as seminars and debates. They cover both theory and practice, e.g. Hungarian language courses for foreigners, with cultural and tourist programmes. Summer universities are attended annually by some 1,200–1,500 students from socialist countries, 600–800 from capitalist countries and about 600 Hungarians. The following are some examples of regular courses: Debrecen Summer University for Hungarian Language and Literature; Szeged Summer University for Teachers; Danube Bend Summer University for Arts at Esztergom; Pécs Summer University for Friendship among Peoples; Salgótarján Summer University for Youth Research; Eger Summer University for the Protection of Monuments; Georgicon Summer University at Keszthely (for agriculture); Sopron Summer University for Nature Preservation.

Professional groups include people having similar interests who wish to expand their knowledge and improve their skills.

The work of *friendship circles* is always associated with some science; the most popular are those for mathematicians, astronomers, physicists, historians, chemists, biologists. The circles of mathematicians have close on 10,000 members, the astronomers almost 6,000.

The number of *specialized courses* rose rapidly in recent years. They resemble school courses, and include foreign languages, courses to develop faculties (e.g. rapid reading); for training specialists in tourism, preparing for university admission, secretarial courses, programming, and so on. Foreign languages are taught on three levels—beginners, advanced and higher. In 1972 close on 40,000 people were taught 16 languages in 2,223 courses,

Service displays are extremely popular, and courses at the Urania Demonstration Observatory in Budapest and the Studio for Natural Sciences are attended by tens of thousands of students.

In 1972 the tourist organization IBUSZ organized 8,200 days of educational tours for groups totalling 187,000 people.

Various social organizations take an active part in general education and in the dissemination of knowledge.

According to the basic principles of socialist cultural policy the trade unions take a generous share in the cultural education of the workers. On the basis of a division of labour with the State bodies they operate in factories, and in the workers' communities, with special regard to the cultural education of the workers at the place of work. They also take care of cultural activities in workers' hostels and holiday homes, in residential areas, in suburban districts and in settlements around industrial units.

They operate partly in their own institutions, partly in public cultural, educational and artistic institutions. They play an important part in drafting the State and social cultural plans and programmes, in assessing them and supervising their execution, and exercise their influence on cultural, artistic, creative processes with due regard to the opinion of working people.

The following is a short summary of the cultural work of trade unions which is referred to in several passages of this booklet in different contexts.

The 453 trade-union cultural homes are visited by 16 million people a year, requiring an annual sum of 206 million forints for maintenance, and for supporting educational activities, professional circles and clubs and language courses. Forty-five thousand lectures yearly have an attendance of 2 million; 2,961 special groups had close on 100,000 members. The forum for regular discussions on politics, economics and public life is attended by half a million workers.

Trade-union libraries in places of work provide access to books for wage and salary earners. Their aggregate stock exceeds 7 million volumes, and the total number of readers is 662,000.

The trade unions support 1,892 amateur artistic groups with a membership of 39,700 who provide some 10,000 programmes a year for domestic audiences. The best groups have also had considerable success in festivals abroad.

The trade unions support adult education in school form, preparatory courses which enable the children of workers and peasants to continue their studies, special groups and vocational advisory services.

The cultural activity of the Hungarian Communist Youth Federation (KISZ) rallying more than 800,000 young people, almost half of the young generation, in their ranks, is a significant factor in Hungarian general education. Cultural work—from local organizations to nation-wide manifestations—is an integral and inseparable part of their activities.

The federation follows with keen interest the cultural development of all categories of Hungarian youth, the ways in which they use their leisure, facilities for education and entertainment; on the other hand it represents the interests of youth in the State and social bodies of management in general education and forwards the demands of the young to the competent cultural authorities. It considers it an important task to arouse and develop cultural demands in youth, to display the variety of culture and self-education, to guide and help the proper utilization of the leisure time of the young, to mobilize young people to take part in various cultural and educational actions.

In conjunction with the movement and with political actions, KISZ organizes cultural manifestations on its own, e.g. cultural meetings, entertainments with programmes preceding World Youth Festivals and also joins in the nation-wide cultural actions, promoting their organization, encouraging their members to participate in large numbers in such manifestations as, for instance, the 'Who knows what?' competitions on television.

It initiated and supported the development of the youth club movement which has formed some 3,000 clubs in recent years. In 1970 these clubs were attended by 3.1 million young people. KISZ takes an active part in the 'Reading People' Movement, including its 'Reading Youth' section, and half of the young generation are now members of libraries.

It helps develop the creative powers of youth and domestic amateur movement in arts. It organizes artistic festivals for university and college students in eight branches of the arts. With the participation of secondary-school pupils it organizes national student days, with programmes by the best amateur choirs, dramatic groups, recital groups and orchestras. It takes part in nation-wide manifestations of different arts, e.g. of the Auróra Recital Competition, and the Choral Festival for Workers and Young Workers. It organizes every year the creative camp of young folk-artists and maintains camps for amateurs in music and the fine arts.

The KISZ Central Artistic Ensemble has, for more than two decades, worked under the supervision of the Central Committee of KISZ and earned recognition abroad; KISZ helps young artists, writers, creators in their career with scholarships, grants and purchases.

The 'Reading People' Movement has co-operated on a wide scale in the organization of the Patriotic People's Front which, in co-operation with the museums and TIT, supports the movement for a deeper knowledge of the country and of each local area. The organization has over 500 branches and their work has resulted in the publication of several studies and monographs, strengthening the patriotic feelings of the young and other categories. The Patriotic People's Front takes part in general education also with its clubs.

The Hungarian National Defence Federation makes a significant contribution to the propagation of technical culture (radio, modelling, mechanics) with its special groups and clubs.

The development of health and physical culture is an important task of the Hungarian Red Cross and of the Health Information Centre whose activities in general education take the form of publications and lectures.

The Federation of Associations for Technical and Natural Sciences and its scientific society also take part in the propagation of scientific knowledge mainly by solving problems requiring higher qualifications and giving professional information to various groups of intellectuals, but their publications are accessible also to the wider public.

Arts and society

A fundamental aim of the arts policy of socialist Hungary is to enable the largest possible number of people to enjoy the widest possible participation in the arts. It intends to prove in practice that the division into 'élite culture' and 'mass culture' is based on a false assumption, and rejects the narrow view that the artistic ideal of the working class in power necessarily means a separate, closed world of proletarian arts.

The guiding principle underlying Hungarian cultural policy, as pointed out earlier, is the hegemony of Marxism in culture. In proportion to their considerable independence, the leaders of the cultural workshops are heavily responsible for the unity of socialist cultural policy, as a centralizing force for the large variety of artistic workshops decentralized throughout the country. In other words, workshops use their own resources for supporting effectively high-standard arts committed to socialist ideology, give scope to valuable humanistic non-socialist creations and to ideological and aesthetic debates on them and prevent the appearance of anti-human, anti-socialist sub-artistic products violating the laws and foreign-political interests of Hungary, destroying taste and arousing base instincts (pornography, horror, etc.).

The implementation of the principles outlined above in publishing and in cultural organization, the central orientation of the institutes of art, and the co-ordination, assessment and approval of their plans and activities is the task of the State authority—the Ministry of Culture. The artistic workshops, critics, artistic forums and the artists themselves are naturally responsible in the last analysis to socialist society for the practical implementation of arts policy, in compliance with the value system and interests of the socialist State.

All arts enjoy substantial State grants in Hungary. The State devotes a constantly growing share of the national income to arts, administering a large part of it to consumers through subsidies to book prices, to theatre, cinema and concert tickets, etc. This system of subsidies gives preference mainly to tendencies serving directly or indirectly the main objectives of socialist society and illustrating the position of the fundamental working classes: revealing current social conflicts in a spirit of socialist alignment, promoting a better and deeper national and social self-knowledge, encouraging the evolution of the socialist way of life and adumbrating the authentic and promising perspectives of socialism with artistic means. In the language of aesthetics this means that the Hungarian forums and institutions of art first of all—but not exclusively—support valuable, contemporary realistic art serving the interest of the society. Beside this, all real humanist artistic values, naturally, enjoy the support of the socialist State.

Never in the troublesome history of Hungary have conditions for creative work been as balanced and advantageous as in the last decade and a half, and perhaps never have creators been as active as now; all significant Hungarian writers and artists of all generations are publicly active, taking part in exhibitions, publishing their writings, including even those whose work was earlier interrupted by periods of enforced silence. A substantial rise in standards, an internal enrichment in all arts could be observed during this period, and at different times in the sixties Hungarian prose, Hungarian cinematic art and also music gave birth to creations outstanding by international standards.

At the same time unprecedently vast sectors of the Hungarian public have come into contact with arts. As to quantity, the greatest contributor has obviously been television. The increasing social interests are attested by the dynamic rise of the number of copies in book publishing, the growing popularity of periodicals, by the success of the movement for the promotion of reading, by the system of spreading subscriptions to operas, cinemas, concerts, by the rise in the number of museum visitors, and by the renewed impetus of the amateur movements in arts. The society finds variegated forms for living up to its role as a patron of arts which express a new content. Social commissions are expected and welcomed by the artists who endorse the objective thus formulated by the tenth Congress of the Hungarian Socialist Workers' Party: let the artists come closer to the masses and let the masses come closer to contemporary, high-quality art.

Support for artistic creation

Artistic creative work is encouraged and supported, and its achievements are popularized in an organized manner through State institutions and social organizations.

The associations of artists organized in the form of unions are meant to promote the undisturbed course and social efficiency of creative work, the healthy evolution of artistic life, the solution of the artists' problems. With a total membership of close to 3,000, Hungarian artists are organized in seven social federations: writers; film and television artists;

actors; dancers; musicians; painters and sculptors; and artist-photographers.

These are voluntary, democratic social organizations of creators. Membership is not a compulsory precondition of artistic activity. The associations take a share in strengthening the contacts between society and art, between artists and the public, enable artists to take part in various forums of public life; and seek the most expedient ways of popularizing art among the masses. It is part of their responsibility to exercise social control over the utilization of funds granted by the State, to attend to the artists, contacts with foreign countries, to delegate members to various cultural institutions (publishers' councils, editorial boards, arts councils, etc.), and to submit recommendations for prize awards. The highest body of each association is the general assembly. This elects a steering committee for the period between two meetings of the general assembly and a secretariat to take charge of administration. The associations are headed by elected chairmen and general secretaries. In some parts of the country they have local groups.

The material conditions for creative work are ensured by the Arts Fund of the Hungarian People's Republic and by other institutions. The members of the Arts Fund may get advances on their work without interest and for long terms. Scholarships are granted to young artists. The fund maintains rest houses and studios for artists in various parts of the country (Balatonföldvar, Galyatetó, Kecskemét, Hódmezóvásárhely, Nagymaros, Szegliget, Zsennye), with about 100 rooms where writers and artists can reside at nominal rates for recreation or creative work. The fund also grants pensions, allowances to retired or low-income members, family, funeral, and emergency allowances. It has nearly 4,000 members.

The Arts Fund is financed from various sources. Art enterprises belonging to the fund (publishing, applied arts, gallery, executive enterprise) pay most of their profits into the fund. Further sources are membership fees, refunds, and the 3 per cent tax on the income derived from the creative activity of artists. The turnover of the Arts Fund is more than 100 million forints a year. Thirty per cent goes in direct subsidies to creative activities of the various departments (fine arts, applied arts, literature, music) according to the number of their members. The annual amount paid out in allowances is 12 to 13 million forints (paid mostly to retired artists). The remaining 70 per cent is devoted to an indirect support of arts (maintenance of institutions, publication of periodicals, building flats and studios, awards, scholarships).

The personal and property rights of authors of scientific, literary and artistic works are protected by law. Any kind of utilization—including the translation—of works of art is allowed only with the prior consent of the author or his legal successor and against the payment of certain sums. Hungary has been a party to the Berne Union since 1922 and a party to the Universal Copyright Convention since 1971.

The tasks of the Office for the Protection of Copyright (Artis Jus), founded in 1953, are to protect Hungarian copyrights at home and abroad as well as to protect foreign authors' rights in Hungary in accordance with obligations assumed. It also takes care of distributing—among Hungarian and foreign authors—royalties deriving from public performances on stage, radio or television, and for such items as gramophone recordings and so on. The Copyright Office is a member of the International Confederation of Associations of Authors and Composers and of the International Bureau of Societies Administering the Rights of Mechanical Recording and Reproduction, and has bilateral contracts with the copyright organizations of their thirty-one Member States. The office promotes international exchanges, publicizes Hungarian works abroad, maintains regular contact with foreign publishing agencies and telecommunication institutions, and makes recommendations regarding its performance of works of foreign authors in Hungary.

Eminent activities and achievements are rewarded by the State with decorations. The award of highest esteem is the Kossuth Prize or the State Prize. These are awarded to those who with their cultural and artistic creations and achievements have made outstanding contributions to the enrichment of socialist culture, literature and arts and thereby enhanced the international esteem and authority of our people, our country and our social system. The Kossuth and State prizes are awarded every third year to artists and other cultural personalities (150,000 forints going with the Grand Prize, 100,000 forints with the first degree, 75,000 forints with the second degree and 50,000 forints with the third). Honorific titles may be bestowed on artists who have attained outstanding merits in developing socialist culture. The first degree is the Eminent Artist of the Hungarian People's Republic, the second is the Merited Artist of the Hungarian People's Republic, which are awarded every year. They entitle the person decorated to a high pension. The prizes and honorific titles are bestowed by the Council of Ministers. Outstanding literary and artistic work as well as eminent performances are rewarded annually by the Minister of Culture literary and artistic prizes: József Attila Prize (literature), Erkel Ferenc Prize (music), Ybl Miklós Prize (architecture), Munkácsy Mihály Prize (fine and applied arts), Liszt Ferenc Prize (music and performing arts), Jászai Mari Prize (dramatic art), Balázs Béla Prize (film). Every year eight to ten artists are decorated in each category. Artistic prizes are also awarded annually by the National Council of the Trade Unions and by most county councils.

Young creators may be granted scholarships (e.g. the Derkovits bursary for young artists awarded for a varying period of time, usually one year). From time to time various institutions invite publishers or periodicals to encourage creative activity and to facilitate the discovery of new talents.

Workshops, forums, literature
and book publishing

For historico-social reasons literature has played an outstanding part in the development of Hungarian culture; for centuries it has acted as a major force in shaping national consciousness. Poetry has for centuries been the leading genre, represented by such prominent creators as Mihály Csokonai Vitéz, Mihály Vörösmarty, Sándor Petőfi, János Arany, Endre Ady, Mihály Babits, Dezső Kosztolányi, Attila József, Miklós Radnóti. Prose and drama have shown a marked development in the twentieth century in the wake of such nineteenth-century writers as Zsigmond Kemény, József Eötvös, Mór Jókai and Kálmán Mikszáth in prose, József Katona and Imre Madách in drama, and prose has become the worthy rival of poetry. The works of lyrical poets like Gyula Illyés, Sándor Weöres, István Vas, Ferenc Juhász, László Nagy, János Pilinszky, Mihály Váci, Sándor Csoóri have been published in, for example, Russian, English, French, German, Italian, Spanish and Czech. In fiction and the short story, world standards are equalled by Zsigmond Móricz, Frigyes Karinthy, Gyula Krudy, Antal Szerb, Endre Gelléri Andor, J. J. Tersánszky, Péter Veres, Tibor Déry, László Németh, Endre Illés, József Lengyel, József Darvas and, in dramatic literature, by Ferenc Molnár, István Örkény, Károly Szakonyi.

The fact-revealing and mind-moulding function of literature is reflected in the development of sociography and of the essay. The best of world literature has been accessible in Hungarian since the late eighteenth century; our eminent writers have always looked upon translating literary works as one of their major tasks.

The literary periodicals have a specific function in displaying recent literary production, in organizing literary life, in the regular information of readers. At present thirteen monthly periodicals and one literary weekly appear in more than 2 million copies a year. Most of them publish the new works of contemporary Hungarian literature; outstanding in this respect are the periodicals *Kortárs* and *Uj Irás*, and the weekly *Élet és Irodalom*. Current world literature is published in Hungarian by the monthly *Nagyvilág*. Besides studies and criticisms regularly published in periodicals, the monthly *Kritika* makes a continuing survey of our entire literary and artistic life. The monthly *Látóhatár* is a digest of the best writing of the Hungarian cultural press.

The social organization of writers is the Association of Hungarian Writers, which has 400 members. The current theoretical and practical problems of literary life are discussed in its departments, organized according to literary categories and in its groups in the provinces. The association has launched a number of important cultural and literary undertakings, as for instance the 'Reading People' Movement whose purpose is to raise the reading standards of the population and increase the number of readers. It started to organize the large-scale literary-sociographic series of books on various aspects and phenomena of Hungarian life (industrialization, professional cultures, development of regional units, changes in the social structure). The circle of young writers also functions within the framework of the Association of Hungarian Writers which also maintains international contacts with foreign organizations of writers.

The collection of written and material items relating to Hungarian literature, their scientific processing and preservation, and the display of the materials processed are the tasks of the central Petőfi Literary Museum which also handles its local collection of minor literary significance. The main fields of its collecting activities cover manuscripts and publications, unpublished writings (diaries, notes, correspondence, documents) and, recently, sound recordings of authors. The museum also collects material relics, objects of use, works of art made by authors, photographs, illustrations to works. Its occasional exhibitions usually coincide with anniversaries. It is the museum's duty to control the memorial houses established in the birthplaces or dwelling places of outstanding authors, writers, etc. Annuals published since 1959 contain reports on its activities and scientific achievements.

The propagation of the best works of Hungarian and foreign literature is a major task of the cultural policy of the Hungarian People's Republic. The State book-publishing enterprises share this task with the periodicals mentioned above.

In Hungary 2,438 books were published in 9,160,000 copies in 1938, as against the 6,648 books in 62,808,000 copies in 1972. This meant about one book per inhabitant in 1938 as against 6.6 in 1972. Books sales have shown a very dynamic rise—10 per cent annually. The value of books sold in 1960 was 554.2 million forints and the corresponding figure for 1972 was 1,217 million forints.

The share of literature in Hungarian book publishing is 11–12 per cent in the number of titles and 23 per cent in the number of copies. The number of works of literature issued annually in Hungary is 730 to 750, each with an average number of copies running into 20,000. Juvenile literature is represented by an annual 230 titles and an average of 28,000 copies.

Book prices in Hungary are very low, as practically all publications are State-subsidized. The price of a 300-page novel, scientific or educational work equals about U.S.$1 when bound. A book of poetry costs about 40 to 60 cents. The real cost price is charged only for entertainment novels. This means, for instance, that a novel by Agatha Christie costs about three time the price of a Hemingway novel. The paperback volumes cost 20 cents.

Volumes of poetry by classical or contemporary Hungarian poets usually have a large circulation. Sándor Petőfi's *Collected Verses*, for instance, were issued in 100,000 copies in recent years, and those of Attila József, in 55,000 copies in 1972. The anthology of contemporary Hungarian poetry *Szép Versek 1971* (Beautiful poems 1971) was published in 1972 in 50,000 copies. Individual volumes of verses by contemporary poets often reach as many as 15,000 to 20,000 copies. Thus, for instance, the volume of verses *Haza a Magasban* by Gyula Illyés, a living classic, attained 17,150 copies in 1972. The average number of copies for new poets varies between 1,500 and 2,000.

The publication of the classics of Hungarian literature in critical editions is the task of the Publishing House of the Hungarian Academy of Sciences. The publishers Magvető and Szépirodalmi are responsible for issuing new authors in the first place, but some other publishers also contribute. Let us quote a few figures just to show the dimensions and proportions: 9,565 works were published in 112 million copies between 1945 and 1972, including more than 10 million copies of Mór Jókai's works, more than 5 million copies of Zsigmond Móricz's works, and Sándor Petőfi's works in over 2 million copies. The forms of publication vary. The series *Magyar Remekírók* (Hungarian Classics) endeavours to include the time-honoured values of Hungarian literature, giving a fuller coverage than any other series before. Other series are devoted to the works of classical writers or of those of the recent past (Mihály Csokonai Vitéz, Sándor Petőfi, János Arany, József Eötvös, Mór Jókai, János Vajda, Kálmán Mikszáth, Endre Ady, Zsigmond Móricz, Lajos Nagy, Attila József, Miklós Radnóti, Pál Szabó, Péter Veres); and of our living writers (József Darvas, Tibor Déry, Endre Illés, Gyula Illyés, József Lengyel, László Németh, István Örkény). Much care is taken in preparing the critical editions of our classics.

Hungarian publication policy is particularly successful in the inexpensive series issued in a large number of copies. Our classics are published in the *Olcsó Könyvtár* (Cheap Library, which is indeed inexpensive: one volume is sold at a price corresponding to two pounds of bread); the best writings of contemporary Hungarian and foreign writers are issued in a new pocket-book series which is enjoying great popularity. Hungarian book publishing gives substantial assistance to young writers.

Almost half of our literary publications are by foreign writers. On the list of countries publishing foreign literature Hungary occupies fourteenth place (*Index Translationum*, vol. 23, 1970). Between 1945 and 1972, 7,899 works of world literature were published in 116 million copies, 75 per cent of these under the auspices of the Europa Book Publishers. About one-third of the literary works translated are by Soviet, English, American and French authors but, of course, the selection covers the literature of the whole world; Hungarian translations are made from forty languages every year.

Over the past twenty-eight years the following authors have been published in more than 1.5 million copies each: Balzac, Gorky, L. Tolstoi and Zola; and in more than 1 million copies: Boccaccio, Victor Hugo, Thomas Mann, Maupassant, Shakespeare, Mark Twain, and Sholokhov. Twentieth-century authors of the Soviet Union and the neighbouring countries, e.g. the Soviets Altmatov, Fadeev, Gaidar, Kataev, Makarenko, Mayakovsky, Paustovsky, Simonov, A. Tolstoi; the Czechs Capek, Hasek and Olbracht; the Poles Newerly and Dambrowska; the Romanians Arghezi and Sadoveanu; the Yugoslavs Andric and Klreza; the Bulgarian Dimov; and the works of Brecht, Seghers and A. Zweig from the German Democratic Republic have run into several editions with a very high number of copies. As to twentieth-century writers of the West, particularly popular among Hungarian readers are Shaw, Maugham, Graham Greene, Golding, Hemingway, Faulkner, Steinbeck, Salinger (English language); Aragon, Simone de Beauvoir, Camus, Merle, Sartre, Vailland, Vercors (French); Böll and Dürrenmatt (German language); Calvino, Moravia and Pratolini (Italian). Our publishers have recently displayed growing interest in the literature of the peoples of Asia, Africa and Latin America.

World literature in Hungarian is also published in numbers of copies and series which make the classics and the contemporary writers accessible to the masses. The series *Classics of World Literature* consists of 150 volumes, while the *Great Works of World Literature* have been sold in subscription in 140,000 copies. In addition, the whole works of Balzac, Chekhov, Dickens, Dostoevsky, Gorky, Hemingway, Victor Hugo, Thomas Mann, Stendhal, Tolstoi, Zola and others are published in a separate series each. Contemporary world literature is presented in the *Europa Zsebkönyvtár* (Pocket Library) in an average of 30,000 to 35,000 copies per volume, and the recent creations of foreign literature are issued in the *Modern Könyvtár* (Modern Library).

An annual almanach of international poetry *Arion* has been published since 1966.

The publication and diffusion of literature are efficiently promoted by various forms of popularization, e.g. the Day of Poetry (on 11 April, birthday of the great proletarian poet Attila József) and the Festival Book Week, in late spring every year. Although the latter concentrates mainly on Hungarian literature, foreign literature is included too. The publishers prepare new and important publications for these traditional occasions; anthologies are sold at reduced prices (50 per cent), literary programmes are organized, writers and readers meet all over the country.

Theatre

Professional theatre began in Hungary almost 200 years ago. The National Theatre, founded in 1837, housed the most diverse kinds for a long time in the capital. Many theatres were built in Budapest and in provincial towns around the turn of the century, and when the theatres were nationalized in 1949, an organization relying on old traditions was adopted to serve socialist ideals of progress.

In the capital—besides the two opera houses—there are seventeen theatres; another fourteen in the provinces brings the total to thirty-one. In addition, the Déryné State Theatre has eight small ensembles which perform all over the country, mainly in towns and villages. Most provincial companies tour regularly within a radius of some fifty kilometres. In 1972 the total number of performances in Hungarian theatres was 15,480 (5,602 in Budapest and 3,976 in the provinces; the Déryné Theatre performed on 1,822 occasions and the number of guest performances of provincial theatres was 4,080).

Most theatres are supervised by the local councils, except for three (the National Theatre, the new experimental '25th Theatre', and the Déryné Theatre) which come under the direct supervision of the Ministry of Culture.

The core of contemporary Hungarian dramatic art consists of present-day Hungarian plays and adaptations of Hungarian literary masterpieces. The annual output is thirty to thirty-five. Repertory theatres mostly play Hungarian authors.

Most new plays and adaptations by Hungarian authors in recent years have been devoted to the relationship between the individual and society, and endeavoured to portray the socialist demands of human life and action. Many analyse the social problems of the present or the recent past. Drawing on the complex politico-ideologico-ethical problems of the fight to build socialism, the new Hungarian drama has revealed the contradictions which hamper progress and tried to show means of coping with them; it has taken a stand, and urged people to take a stand, on such issues as, for example, how to live a life worthy of man, how to enrich our demands by spiritual and moral values, how the empty manifestations of the petty-bourgeois way of life can be overcome (József Darvas, *A Térképen nem Található* (Not on the Map); Endre Fejes, *Rozsdatemető* (Scrapyard); Gyula Illés, *Bölcsek a Fán* (Wisemen on the Tree); Akos Kertész, *Makra*; István Örkény, *Macskajáték* (Cat Game); Károly Szakonyi, *Adáshiba* (Defective Transmission); László Németh, *Nagy Család* (Big Family); *Villámfénynél* (Lit by Lightning), *Papucshős* (Henpecked Husband)).

Another group of the works staged presents the progressive, revolutionary periods and prominent figures of Hungarian history or historical situations outside of Hungary. Most also examine the effects—social and ethical—of human behaviour, reminding us of the responsibility of man and society committed to progress, and the importance of the unity of the progressive forces, pinpointing the dramatic conflicts of man fighting and creating values (László Gyurkó, *Szerelmen, Elektra* (Elektra, My Love), *Don Quijote*; Gyula Illés, *Fáklyaláng* (Torchlight), *Tizsták* (The Pure), *Testvérek* (Brothers), *Malom a Séden* (Mill on the Séd); László Németh, *Áruló* (Traitor)).

All classics of world literature from the Greek dramas to the present day can be seen on the Hungarian stage. The most popular authors are Chekhov, Gorky, Molière and Shakespeare and also József Katona, Imre Madács, Mihály Vörösmarty, Ede Szigligeti and Sándor Bródy.

Particular attention is paid to the masterpieces of socialist dramatic literature, the Soviet classics, the living Soviet writers, Brecht and the drama output of the friendly socialist countries (for example, Gorky's works; Lunacharsky, *Don Quijote*; Kataev, *A Kör Négyszögesítése* (Squaring the Circle); Babel, *Alkony* (Sunset); Vasiliev, *Csendesek a Hajnalok* (The Dawns are Quiet); Aitmatov, *A versenyló halála* (Death of the Race Horse); almost all Brecht's works; Baranga, *Közvélemény* (Public Opinion); Kruczkowsky, *A Szabadság Elsö Napja* (First Day of Freedom); Krlezsa, *Glembay L.T.D.* and *Léda*; Radoev, *Rómeó, Julia és a Benzin* (Romeo, Juliet and Petrol)).

A wide range of Western plays can be seen on Hungarian stages, including Dürrenmatt, Hochuth, Arthur Miller, Weiss, Tennessee Williams (e.g. Dürrenmatt, *Visit of the Old Lady*; Miller, *View from the Bridge* and *Death of a Salesman*; Weiss, *Marat-Sade* and *Investigation*; Hochuth, *Regent*; Tennessee Williams, *A Streetcar Named Desire*, and *Glass Menagerie*). Operettas, musicals and musical comedies enjoy a vast popularity.

The annual number of theatre-goers approaches the 5 million mark in Hungary, which has a population of 10 million.

A large part of the audiences (41.7 per cent) finds access to the theatre through the entertainment services of the trade unions, and another part is composed of permanent subscribers. In 1972, 52,000 of the Budapest audiences were subscribers; in the provincial theatres there were 99,000. Great importance is attached to youth. In addition to the State Puppet Theatre, the capital has a theatre for children, and considerable reductions on ticket prices are granted to students and to young people working in industries and agriculture. Of all the performances in 1972, 2,667 were for the young; one-fifth of all theatre-goers, i.e. 1 million spectators, were young people.

There is wide range of stylistic variety in Hungarian dramatic art. Outstanding artistic personalities still represent noble conservative tendencies while others follow a post-naturalistic style of contemporary ideology. Many are partisans of the Stanislavsky method, perhaps with some modifications, and others carry on Reinhardt's teachings, total theatre, the earlier or recent traditions and achievements of the Brechtian theatre; the circus theatre; recent expressionistic, political theatrical endeavours have also eminent representatives. All in all, experiments give a more contemporary shape to the contact between public and artist.

Engaged on a contractual basis by the companies are about 900 actors. Hungary maintains the repertory system, which means that theatres have permanent companies of actors engaged for at least one year but usually for longer.

In 1972–73, eighty-three actors and eighteen stage managers were trained in the four classes of the College for Dramatic and Cinematic Art.

The Association of Hungarian Theatrical Art has five sections (theatre managers, stage managers, playwrights, producers, actors); theoretical problems are discussed and conferences and study tours arranged. Hungary is a member of the International Theatre Institute and the International Association of Theatre for Children and Young People.

The Hungarian Theatre Institute, founded in 1957, is engaged in studying the history of Hungarian theatre. It has its own museum, and provides Hungarian theatres with information about theatres elsewhere. It issues a bulletin in three languages.

Its monthly *Szinház* (Theatre) publishes theoretical articles and analytical criticisms. The weekly *Film, Szinház, Muzsika* (Film, Theatre, Music) is a popular magazine.

Music

Prior to 1945 Hungarian music was poorly organized and relied on a narrow public. After the liberation new demands and interests were aroused among people earlier excluded from culture. Budapest has a leading position in the national development of Hungarian musical life. With its two opera houses, several musical institutions, eight professional orchestras and other art ensembles, it has become a centre of domestic musical activities and international musical life.

The opera and concert network is the most important in the institutional pattern. Prior to 1945 the country had one single opera house. In 1972–73, the 500 performances of the 1,050 strong company of the two theatres of the Hungarian State Opera House in Budapest were attended by 650,000 people. In addition, the 300 artists of the three opera companies established in the provinces since the liberation organized 257 performances for 167,000 spectators in fifteen towns. The Déryné State Theatre performs comic operas in villages which are arranged to suit special purposes and local conditions.

The Országos Filharmonia (National Philharmonic Orchestra) arranges concerts in Budapest and throughout the country. It organized 2,000 concerts in 1972 (half of them for juvenile audiences) in 231 premises, attended by 871,000 people. The number of professional symphonic orchestras has grown from one before 1945 to thirteen in 1973. The major symphonic orchestras (e.g. State Concert Orchestra, Hungarian Radio and Television Orchestra, Philharmonic Society) and the Hungarian State Opera have had considerable success in other countries in Europe and in other continents.

Both concert and opera performances rely largely on the subscription system, most of the audiences holding season tickets, including young people, who enjoy substantial discounts. There are many special performances for young workers.

Programmes include the best of the past and present. The Opera House features contemporary Hungarian and foreign compositions in series. In addition to Ferenc Erkel, Béla Bartók and Zoltán Kodály's works, the State Opera stages new operas every year. Sándor Szokolay's *Blood Wedding* has earned international recognition; similarly Khachaturyan and Seregi's ballet *Spartacus*. More and more contemporary operas are shown in the two opera houses of Budapest and in the three in provincial towns. (Some of those shown in the capital are Berg's *Wozzeck* and *Lulu*, Shostakovich's *Katerina Izmailova*, Britten's *Peter Grimes*, *Albert Herring* and *Midsummer Night's Dream*; in the provinces: Hindemith's *Mathis the Painter*, Einem's *Danton's Death* and the *Visit of the Old Lady*, Prokofiev's *The Love of Three Oranges*). In 1972 new Hungarian orchestral compositions were played for the first time on 183 occasions, new solo and chamber music on 455 occasions. Much contemporary foreign music is also played.

Musical publishing houses have recently been established for the first time. The record factory Hungaroton annually records 2,500 minutes of serious music (over 20 per cent of its total output). The turnover in records of serious music trebled between 1968 and 1972 (538,000 in 1972). Hungaroton's major undertakings include the complete works of Bartók, selected works of Kodály, and the best works of Hungarian performing artists. By 1973 Hungaroton records had won fifteen grand prizes abroad.

The Edition Musical Budapest doubled the number of copies of its musical publications between 1970 and 1972 (365,000 volumes in 1972). The number of copies of 638 scores published in 1972 runs to 1,558,000 (mostly Hungarian compositions and music for teaching). The organization of performances of Hungarian music abroad is an integral part of the publisher's activities.

Creative work in music is encouraged by substantial State subsidies. The Music and Dance Art Department of the Ministry of Culture commissions operatic, symphonic, chamber and choral works and encourages their performance. Creation is promoted also by tenders, by scholarships at home and abroad; substantial State support is given to performing musicians.

The Ferenc Liszt Academy of Music, an institute of higher education, trains students in all branches of music. In 1972–73, 769 students were taught by 361 teachers in the academy and in the six teacher-training sections. Most students pay no tuition fees and receive grants. Young musicians are given assistance in the form of scholarships and opportunities for performances.

Through the International Concert Board Hungarian performing artists maintain close contact with the musical life of the world. The figures for 1972 are: 377 solo musicians and small groups performed abroad on 1,258 occasions, and the 34 major ensembles gave 34 performances; 192 foreign artists appeared 541 times before Hungarian audiences and 14 major ensembles gave 39 performances. International music competitions help the development of young musicians: 807 entered for Budapest competitions between 1956 and 1971. Between 1952 and June 1973, Hungarian musicians won 31 first prizes and 249 other prizes in international competitions at home and abroad. Among the outstanding names are conductors János Ferencsik and György Lehel, pianist Annie Fischer, violinist Dénes Kovács; the Bartok and Kodály string quartets have also had considerable international success. Hungarian composers widely known and successful at home and abroad include Sándor Balassa, Zsolt Durkó, Ferenc Farkas, Pál Kadosa, György Kurtág, György Ránki and András Szöllősy.

The Musicological Institute of the Hungarian Academy of Sciences has twenty-two permanent staff and many commissioned research workers. Attached to the institute are the Bartók Archives which conserve Bartók's heritage in Hungary. One of the institute's most important publications, the *Corpus Musicae Popularis Hungaricae*, is a comprehensive collection of thematically classified Hungarian folk songs, collected by Béla Bartók and Zoltán Kodály. Nine musical periodicals reflect the development of musicology in Hungary; the best known are *Muzsika* and *Magyar Zene*. A part of *Film, Szinház, Muzsika* is also devoted to music.

Festivals, celebrations, international courses and free universities are essential public features of musical life. There are festivals in twelve towns, and four international musical courses are regularly organized (the Budapest Bartók Seminar, the Kecskemét Károly Seminar, the Pécs Camp of Musicians and the Esztergom Camp of Musicians).

The Association of Hungarian Musicians has 205 members who are among the most eminent representatives of Hungarian musical life. The association is a member of the International Music Council and other international societies. Operating under its aegis is the Hungarian Jeunesses Musicales, with 5,000 members, which promotes extracurricular musical education for young people.

Dance

Before 1945 there was one single dance company with a few members, while in 1973 there were several professional ensembles, representing different artistic trends.

The ballet company of the Hungarian State Opera House, with its 110 dancers and 120 performances a year, can rightly be called the national repertory dance theatre. Its programmes include romantico-classical ballets, major creations of Soviet ballet, choreographic presentations of significant twentieth-century Hungarian music, and some outstanding West European ballets.

The thirty-strong contemporary Ballet Sopianae (at the National Theatre in Pécs) has a few Baroque ballets (music and dance) in its repertory but concentrates mainly on music and choreography from the second half of our century.

Folklore is represented by four professional dance companies, with 25 to 45 members each, who give 90 to 120 performances each annually. Each has its own orchestra, and two have choirs. The best known is the Hungarian State Folk Ensemble. Besides folklore they also provide contemporary dramatic and symphonic dance compositions. Over the past 15–20 years they too have had considerable success abroad.

The dancers engaged by the ballet and folk dance companies are trained in the State Ballet Institute in two courses which take four and nine years respectively. The institute is now over twenty years old.

State support mainly takes the form of commissions, contributions to the cost of staging, and awards to authors and performers of new works.

Professional artists (e.g. ballet masters, choreographers, teachers, dancers) and people who do research are included among the 230 members of the Association of Hungarian Dance Artists, which acts in an advisory capacity to authorities, theatres and companies, and issues a regular bulletin on Hungarian and international dance.

Film

The Hungarian film world—nine enterprises and one institute—is supervised by the Film Directorate of the Ministry of Culture but cinemas are supervised by the cultural sections of the local councils.

Feature films are produced by two autonomous studios (Budapest and Hunnia) which make twenty to twenty-two films annually. Upon its own initiative or in collaboration with foreign partners, the Ponnonia Film Studio produces animated cartoons and puppet films, and takes care of title printing and dubbing.

The following are some figures on Hungarian film production for 1972: 20 feature films (15 in colour); 104 feature films commissioned by television; 79 newsreels; 26 documentaries; 19 popular-scientific; 44 educational; 105 propaganda and publicity; 42 films and newsreels on national defence.

The Balázs Béla young film actors' studio turned out fifteen films in 1972.

The Pannonia Studio dubbed 83 long and 130 short films for television, and 63 long films for cinemas; subtitled 110 long films and produced 35 animated feature films, 29 puppet films (28 for television), 35 publicity films and 20 other types.

Over the past ten years Hungarian cinema has been substantially enriched in both content and form, and has had much international success (mainly new feature films). Underlying this recognition is the unequivocal affirmation of socialist and human progress. Hungarian feature films diversely and authoritatively depict Hungarian life in the present and recent past, the life, achievements and difficulties of working class people building socialism (Péter Bacsó, *Jelenidő* (Present Tense) and *Harmadik Nekifutás* (The Third Onset); Zoltán Fábry, *Kőrhinta* (Merry-go-round) and *Husz Óra* (Twenty Hours); István Gaál, *Sodrásban* (Carried by the Current); András Kovács, *Nehéz Emberek* (Difficult People); Károly Makk, *Megszállottak* (The Obsessed); Sándor Sára, *Feldobott Kő* (Stone Tossed): István Szabó, *Apa* (Daddy)) or have contributed to the formation of a realistic national consciousness (Miklós Jancsó, *Szegénylegények* (Outlaws); Ferenc Kósa, *Tizezer Nap* (Ten Thousand Suns); András Kovács, *Hideg Napok* (Cold Days)).

These and other themes (for example adaptations of classical Hungarian literary works: *Egri Csillagok* (Stars of Eger), *Szindbád*, etc.) have been screened in the new Hungarian film idiom which has enriched the traditions of classical cinema and assimilated fertile ideas from Soviet film and from *cinéma vérité*.

The cinema network consists of 3,756 cinemas (12 with 70 mm, 1,044 with 35 mm, and 2,700 with 16 mm) of which 2,713 have wide screens.

The number of cinema-goers in 1972 was 74,391,471, including 15.7 per cent viewers of Hungarian films. The 160–70 films shown annually include Soviet, Czechoslovak, German, Polish, Romanian, Yugoslav, American, British, French, Italian and Scandinavian films.

The low prices of seats are part of cultural policy (the average costing less than 2 kilograms of bread).

Film reviews are held every year or two. For example, the biennial Feature Film Review at Pécs assesses the Hungarian film output over a given period from the angle of cultural and political objectives. The annual Miskolc Festival of Hungarian short films helps to publicize documentary, publicity and popular science films and animated cartoons, and to attract amateurs of short films. The Youth Film Days held biennially at Kőszeg show films made for or by youth, and also offer an opportunity to assess the development of contacts, through film clubs, between young actors and the public.

A four-year course is provided for film and television directors and cameramen at the College of Dramatic and Cinematic Art whose democratic internal life promotes the socialist ideological development of young film artists and gives them chances to experiment and develop their talents.

The Hungarian Institute of Cinematology and Film Archives covers the following: research; promotion of knowledge about the cinema (film museum, film clubs); publishing of theoretical, historical and popular works, including a periodical (*Filmkultura*); collection of films (acquisition and preservation, processing of films, selection and publishing of documents, film library).

Three periodicals deal with the cinema. *Filmkultura* (7,000 copies) provides analytical criticism and a liaison between film makers and their public. The fortnightly *Filmvilág* carries information and criticism. *Film, Szinház, Muzsika*, a weekly, has been already mentioned.

The considerable favourable balance of Hungarian film exports over imports is largely due to successes at various film festivals. In 1972 they were entered in fifty-seven international festivals and won thirty prizes and diplomas (Cannes, Cracow, Karlovy Vary, Locarno).

The arts

Hungarian fine arts are in a dynamic period of growth and change. The year of liberation, 1945, was a milestone also in the history of the fine arts, which took a decisive turn as far as their social role, existential foundations and the relationship between artist and public are concerned.

This process affected the essential structure of the arts, and produced genres capable of concentrating and of widely diffusing the ideals of the community. It gave a tremendous impetus to the monumental arts and the use of sculptural groups in public places, decorative architecture, mural painting, mosaics, tapestry. These reflect the collective aspects of Hungarian art. State funds encourage artists to produce works which can be made accessible to all and become the intellectual property of the entire society.

Artists are invited to submit paintings, sculpture, graphic art and work in various branches of the applied arts. These invitations are periodically followed by State purchases, made upon the recommendations of committees of artists and experts. The purchases are exhibited in the modern collections of museums, in houses of culture and cultural institutions, and in exhibitions at home and abroad.

Besides the State as patron of arts, a growing number of social institutions, county and town councils, industrial and agricultural enterprises provide financial support.

Contemporary Hungarian fine and applied arts are characterized by endeavours to find new ways and means suitable for expressing our age and society. Trends dating from between the two world wars have amalgamated and formed progressive traditions, which ensure room for experiment as well as a kind of continuity. The main course of development consists of variations on modern realism, but most recent works, combining the effects of current international trends with domestic traditions, have also a place and a public.

Our society turns with particular attention to the relationship between art and the public. The raising of the standards of visual education—especially for the understanding of twentieth-century art—imposes a difficult task on the organizations concerned. Many Hungarian institutions—like the Association of Hungarian Fine Arts, the College of Fine Arts, the Institute for Culture—are intensively engaged in developing visual culture.

Painters and sculptors have also realized the importance of contacts between art and the public. Individual and collective exhibitions are held all over the country and enjoy a popularity which is marked by large attendances.

The Department of Fine Arts in the Ministry of Culture is concerned with the problems of contemporary arts. It relies on different institutions.

The central State authority passing judgement on contemporary works of art in Hungary is the Fine Arts and Applied Arts Jury, founded in 1964. Among its most important functions are to encourage the creation of works of fine and applied arts that reflect the constructive life of the country, and to appraise works from the artistic angle, and as possible items for exhibitions organized from State funds. Relying on various State and social bodies, the jury has set up permanent committees in collaboration with artists and members of the Association of Hungarian Artists. The jury awards commissions, invites tenders for monumental works of art, and recommends the allocation of the necessary funds.

The organization called *Exhibition Institutions* (Art Gallery) arranges exhibitions at State level in Budapest, elsewhere in Hungary, and abroad. Much of the expenditure is covered from State subsidies; a small part comes from the organization's own income. It is the keeper of the Ministry of Culture collection of fine and applied arts which increases from year to year through purchases, and collaborates in showing items from the collection at home and abroad.

The Applied Arts Council controls the artistic standard of industrial mass products and maintains contacts with domestic and foreign organizations having similar tasks.

The Fine Arts Section of the Arts Fund is responsible for providing material conditions for creative work. It maintains workshops for casting bronze, dressing stone, duplicating, and it arranges sales. Profits are used to finance allowances and services for the members of the fund.

The Association of Hungarian Fine Arts is the highest professional and social organization of Hungarian painters and sculptors. It is responsible for supporting creative work and assisting the State authorities in purchasing objects of art, awarding State commissions, making critical assessments, and arranging exhibitions and publicity.

The diploma awarded by the Faculty of Painting, Sculpture, Graphic Art and Restoration at the Hungarian College of Fine Arts qualifies for teaching and other assignments. Talented graduates may continue with a three-year post-graduate course which is most helpful to their artistic development.

There is a four-year course at the Hungarian College of Applied Arts in Budapest for ceramists, gold- and silversmiths, textile artists, designers, interior decorators and model designers.

AMATEUR ARTISTS

Socialist cultural policy regards amateur artistic activities as pastimes but also recognizes their educational value to the individual and to the community, and grants them institutional support.

Active members of amateur groups assimilate the artistic and cultural content of what they recreate and interpret for an audience. The audience in turn enhances its aesthetic receptivity and taste, while both learn to appreciate the great works of art, music and literature. The groups play a significant part in education for collective life. Identical artistic interests

TABLE 1

	Groups	Members		Groups	Members
Choirs	1,298	37,251	Art groups	364	7,082
Orchestras	1,327	13,453	Film circles	177	6,810
Drama and literary			Social dance, ballet	999	32,145
groups	2,256	34,268	Other	490	11,014
Puppet groups	366	5,737	Groups in factories		
Folk ensembles	210	5,167	and enterprises	679	10,860
Folk-dance groups	943	16,127	TOTAL	9,109	179,914

develop a spirit of solidarity and contribute to the formation of socialist collective behaviour.

The social significance of the amateur movement is also conditioned by its contacts with progressive political movements. These contacts are rooted in the anti-capitalist feelings of workers. After the liberation the amateur artistic movements, in accordance with our cultural policy, have always provided solid ground for contacts between committed art and the masses.

In 1971, the number of amateur art groups and circles was 9,109, with a membership of 179,914. The number functioning in cultural institutions maintained by the councils, the trade unions and other organizations is shown in Table 1.

The educational significance of groups is shown by the fact that the members spend an average of 200 hours a year together on rehearsals and other occasions. Their popularity with the public can be realized when we consider that in 1971, for instance, there were 19,046 performances for audiences totalling 3,586,888.

Artistic standards are, naturally, not homogeneous. The leading groups number between 300 and 350 (20 to 60 for each branch of art). They boast significant productions, receive wide attention from critics, are considered for national and international festivals, undertake guest performances in the provinces, suburbs, farmsteads, and hostels. They are generally not satisfied with copying ready-made models, but try to explore new ways and means of expression, often composing or writing their own works. They make bold experiments in new genres.

The amateur movement has made great strides in recent years, raising standards and enriching artistic forms. Choirs have the longest traditions, and have won a number of prizes at festivals abroad. They perform contemporary and classical choral music, and old and new revolutionary songs. A television contest called 'Fly, Peacock!' started a folk-song renaissance a few years ago. Amateur instrumental groups reach standards which reflect the internationally recognized standards of the network of music schools in Hungary.

Amateur theatricals have also greatly developed. Relying on workers' and students' drama traditions, the amateur theatre has evolved a colourful repertory and a specific style of acting, performing mainly documentary plays on topical public issues, popular comedies, musical programmes, oratorios. The puppet theatres are notable for the noble quality of the literary and musical material used. Folk dance has relied on the contemporary staging of folklore to express the emotional and intellectual world of our own days. Rejuvenated folklore and modern theatrical production have jointly contributed to substantial successes abroad and to domestic culturo-political achievements in the folk-dance movement.

The Institute for Culture is responsible for a large variety of tasks which include organizing and controlling the fundamental and extension training of the leaders of theatre, folk dance and other groups, and co-ordinating the work of amateur ensembles that are supported by State and social organizations. It supervises the arrangement of festivals and professional and artistic standards.

The amateur festivals provide important forums where criticism can assess achievements and encourage further development. The best representatives of every branch of art—choirs, folk-dance groups, film clubs—take part and meet ensembles and creators from socialist and Western countries. The amateur drama movement became a member of the International Amateur Theatre Association in 1973. Besides national and international festivals each amateur branch has its regional and local—annual or biennial—festivals. A considerable impetus and wide publicity has been given to the movement by the Hungarian Radio and Television Services.

ART EDUCATION IN THE SCHOOL

The foundations of artistic education are laid in the kindergarten where play is used to acquaint children 3–6 years old with the aesthetic aspects of reality and arouse a desire for beauty in them.

For the 6–14 age group schooling is compulsory. The curricula in all eight grades include artistic education: singing and music for one hour a week in the first grade and two hours beginning with the second; drawing is taught for one or two hours a week as from the second grade.

These subjects prepare the way: drawing 'should make the pupils see the characteristic features of surrounding reality and teach them to portray it realistically'; singing and music 'should give a foundation to their sense of musical mother tongue'.

In the higher grades music and drawing are aesthetically linked with other subjects such as literature.

By the end of the eighth grade this training should '. . . enable the pupils to love arts, willingly to visit museums and exhibitions, . . . induce them to realize the aesthetic points of view in their environment on a level corresponding to their age', while 'music with its means and rich power of arousing emotions should contribute to the development of the moral characteristics . . . of the pupils'.

Hungary has 134 general schools with music and singing sections, attended by 25,000 pupils. State music schools provide training for another 50,000 in 200 towns and villages.

Both types of school use the Kodály system which incorporates Zoltan Kodály's educational ideas. Its essential features are as follows:

The development of a homogeneous musical mother tongue and culture by concentrating on singing, on a curriculum consisting of folk music, and Hungarian and universal music.

A conscious use of the educational possibilities of music in forming a versatile and well-balanced personality.

Devoting adequate attention not only to professional musical training but also to the musical education of audiences.

There have been two types of secondary schools since 1961: grammar schools and trade schools.

The number of hours devoted weekly to general culture subjects varies according to type and grade.

Singing and music are taught once a week in all grammar schools and all grades, so that pupils learn how to sing and how to listen to music, i.e. receive a practical musical education based on a minimum of theoretical knowledge.

Drawing is taught in the first grade two hours a week. The curriculum of the fourth (last) grade includes the analysis of works of art, which deals with the role and purpose of art, the aesthetics of industrial forms, objects used in daily life and of decorative elements, the artistic characteristics of photography, of the cinema and television.

Cinema aesthetics has been taught for a decade in both types of secondary school—six to ten hours a year are spent discussing the idiom and the basic aesthetics of the cinema. The curricula of the third and fourth grades comprise film analysis. Prior to 1968, pupils were shown films in afternoon performances that were discussed next day in class. School television now handles both the projection and the discussion of films, and broadcasts every programme twice.

Some schools have classes with specialized curricula which may devote an additional three to four hours a week to musical and visual education.

Schools for outstanding talents include grammar schools for singing and music, middle school for fine and applied arts, and the State Ballet Institute.

Admission to these schools is restricted by an entrance examination. The schools provide theoretical and practical training.

The purpose of education in the aesthetics of art is to give the pupil a more comprehensive and rich acquaintance with the world and help him to assimilate it, to create a conscious and active link between the pupil and the world, to enable him to search for beauty, to be attracted by it, to be receptive of it, and to enjoy it—in other words, its purpose is the creation of beautiful works, and the moulding of aesthetic attitudes and ways of life.

The educational programme makes a detailed analysis of the forms of artistic education which can best be used at each age, and suggests activities that offer rich experiences and ways of retaining and deepening the experiences acquired.

In vocational secondary schools extracurricular art education is provided through study circles, visits to theatres and museums, and through choirs and theatrical groups.

The following institutions of higher education train artists: the College of Fine Arts; the College of Applied Arts; the Ferenc Liszt College of Music; the College of Dramatic and Cinematic Art.

Radio, television, the press

Mass communications can provide access to culture for millions if cultural policy and its implementation open this access as widely as possible to readers, listeners and viewers. In addition to their political function, socialist-type mass communications have the cultural purpose of preserving and spreading national and universal cultural values, promoting new works, using art criticism to guide artists and help the public to understand what they produce and finally, in the widest sense of the term, raising the cultural standards of the public, and improving taste.

The general principles of our cultural policy outlined in the introduction also apply to mass communications, but have certain features which apply little or not at all to the more traditional world of theatres, exhibitions, concerts and book publishing.

These features derive from the fact that the mass media are addressed to millions of people. Consequently, they must tackle the problems of selection and processing in a way different from that in which, for example, an experimental theatre would for an audience that may not exceed 100. They must also try to differentiate for various sectors of the public. Hungarian mass media usually reckon with four sectors in matters of art: first, the narrowest group, of creators and performers; secondly, the connoisseurs; thirdly, those who have only just started to get acquainted or become familiar with art; fourthly, a broad group who know little or nothing about art, but who can be introduced to it through the mass media.

Radio and television

The cultural and artistic policies of Hungarian radio and television are not only closely linked with the national cultural policy and with the principles outlined above, but are also strongly co-ordinated with one another (with due regard of course to the particular features of each and the somewhat different public for which each caters).

Apart from programme policy, both have to bear in mind the vast possibilities and possible drawbacks that derive from the technico-institutional conditions of electronic mass communication.

Besides reproducing and transmitting, electronic mass communication is an autonomous branch of art because it has its own specific ways of approaching reality and of contacting the public which are different from those of the other arts. Its own works thus contribute to the cultural values of society.

Hungarian Radio and Television give some 200 original radio plays, television plays and films in a year; some 100 symphonic and world premieres of chamber and choral works.

The main objection to culture via the mass media is that the audience is more passive and the attention is more divided than when the medium is a book, theatre, cinema, or live concert. But the operation need not be passive. If the social institutions (school, family, political structures) teach the citizens to be active and conscious, then culture via the mass media may also be active, conscious and selective.

Some 40 to 50 per cent of the audience are in fact selective in their attitude to programmes.

Moreover there is also direct and positive assimilation. For example, not only did the television series *Fly, Peacock!* teach some beautiful folk-songs to millions of spectators, but the teams preparing for competitions discovered hundreds of folk-songs formerly unknown in the country of Bartók and Kodály where one would have thought no folk-song could have been overlooked. The radio series *This Side of the Tisza—Beyond the Danube* and the television game *Black and White* have directly acquainted the whole nation with counties, districts and provinces, and stimulated the competing teams to reveal the history of their places of residence, their native land.

Another aspect to be considered in programme policy is that the mass media create prestige; the mere fact of appearing in front of a camera enhances authority. There is almost invariably a sharp rise in the demand, for example, for a book described, shown or adapted on television—or even as soon as its forthcoming appearance on television is announced.

In some cases, however, there is a certain amount of opposition to what some kinds of listener or viewer regard as highbrow. This problem has to be approached tactfully.

Hungarian Radio and Television relies on several methods:

Programmes that mix highbrow and more evidently entertaining items.

Extremely popular artists are brought in to perform works which are complicated or difficult to understand.

The principle of gradual assimilation, e.g. beat, followed by folk, leading up to certain trends in modern music; or romantic prose to introduce realism which, in turn, may introduce modern prose.

A consistent educational effort to teach ordinary listeners to decode systems of artistic signs, and acquire the skills of a connoisseur.

However, this policy does not attempt to foster illusions, and emphasizes, implicitly and explicitly, that culture simply cannot be acquired without effort or be presented as a gift.

RADIO

On 31 December 1972, the number of radio subscribers exceeded 2.5 million, i.e. an average of 76 per cent of families had radios (85 per cent in Budapest, 79 per cent in provincial towns, 69 per cent in villages). The number of receivers per licensee rose from 1.15 in 1967 to 1.5 in 1972; in Budapest, 20 per cent have three or more radios, the corresponding figures being 10 per cent for provincial towns and 5 per cent for villages.

The time devoted to listening has also increased in recent years. In 1967 the adult population spent 88 minutes a day listening to the radio; by 1972 it was 144 minutes. Entertainment, news and magazine programmes are the most popular, but many educational and art programmes have large audiences. The short daily educational musical item *Who Wins Today?* is heard by some 30 per cent of all listeners. Masterpieces of world theatre attract 10 to 20 per cent; Racine's *Phaedre*, by no means an easily digestible play, recently attracted 9 per cent.

In 1972 more than 1 million programme minutes were broadcast through the three central transmitters. The five provincial transmitters broadcast programmes of 1–2 hours daily. Time on the two central programmes was divided as follows: 37 per cent light music; 20 per cent serious music; 13 per cent entertainment; 3 per cent educational; 3 per cent sport; 4 per cent other.

TELEVISION

On 31 December 1972 there were over 2 million television licences, i.e. 62 per cent of the population (69 per cent in Budapest, 69 per cent in provincial towns and 55 per cent in villages). In 1967 the adult population spent an average of 50 minutes viewing on days of broadcasting. This rose to 76.1 minutes in 1969 and to 86.4 in 1972. There are large audiences, especially at peak hours, when even educational quizzes (e.g. the series *Who Knows What?*) engage the attention of over 80 per cent of listeners, and in 1972, the last episode of a series on *The Odyssey* had 83 per cent. Even science education items (e.g. *Delta*) broadcast outside peak hours, regularly attract about 30 per cent. In 1972, literary or musical features and commemorative series like *We are Tracing Petőfi* or *The Zoltán Kodály Song Competition*—again outside peak hours—also attracted about 30 per cent.

In 1972 Hungarian Television broadcast 169,000 programme minutes in the first and in the second experimental (partly colour) programmes. There is no transmission on Mondays (reserved for other kinds of entertainment). Programme proportions in 1971 were: 27 per cent political; 14 per cent serious entertainment; 41 per cent light entertainment; 15 per cent educational; and 3 per cent juvenile.

The share of home-made productions is rather high: 60 per cent. But even the 40 per cent imports include many Hungarian-foreign co-productions. Every year Hungarian television features 'national days', when programmes are jointly composed with foreign television companies to give an insight to the daily life of other countries. With a few exceptions, foreign productions are dubbed.

The press

Each of the five central and nineteen county dailies has a cultural column. The five central newspapers are as follows: *Népszabadság*, central organ of the Hungarian Socialist Worker's Party; *Magyar Hirlap*, a political daily; *Népszava*, central organ of the Hungarian Trade Unions; *Magyar Nemzet*, organ of the Patriotic People's Front; *Esti Hirlap*, political daily of the Budapest Committee of the Hungarian Socialist Workers' Party.

The average daily paid circulation was 1,452,000 in the first half of 1973 (738,000 *Népszabadság*, 49,000 *Magyar Hirlap*, 281,000 *Népszava*, 117,000 *Magyar Nemzet*, 267,000 *Esti Hirlap*).

In general the dailies devote a page or a page and a half to culture every day, and more in week-end issues, which even have supplements. Twelve pages of the Sunday supplement of *Népszabadság* are devoted largely to cultural problems, four pages of the Saturday supplement of *Népszava*, and four pages of the Saturday supplement of *Magyar Hirlap*. Many county dailies also publish supplements.

Népszabadság, *Népszava*, *Magyar Hirlap* and regional newspapers publish poetry, short stories and literary sociography in their weekend numbers and supplements. They thus try to keep pace with developments in cultural life, draw attention to the most important events and productions, and mobilize the masses to take part in the cultural tasks ahead.

The cultural column of *Népszabadság* fulfils the important educational task of reporting on and assessing the latest in literary, film, dramatic, musical and artistic work. Its descriptive and analytic articles and reports associate individual subjects with issues of national and general education. The paper regularly devotes articles to cultural policy, workers' education, the cultural needs of youth, cultural homes and libraries, amateur movements and the dissemination of knowledge.

Magyar Hirlap often devotes its editorial or full-page articles and series to cultural problems of national significance. In 1972 it published all articles relevant to the debate on visual culture. It reports on art workshops and publishes a weekly technical and scientific supplement. Reports and articles analyse ways and means of providing lifelong education, facilities

66

for general education in different types of settlement, co-operation between various institutions of education, the division of labour and extent of co-operation between the State and social organizations concerned with culture.

Népszava as the organ of the trade unions concentrates in the first place on the cultural life of the workers. Its cultural supplement appearing on Saturdays is regularly devoted to topical questions of workers' education, whereas its youth supplement analyses the social issues of the cultural life of the younger generation. The daily gives useful advice for making good use of the growing hours of leisure.

Magyar Nemzet often examines current problems of spreading knowledge and the cultural position of the intelligentsia. It discusses general education and the protection of artistic monuments, and endeavours to carry on the tradition of progressive humanistic culture. One of its specific tasks is to keep interest alive in the cultivation of the mother tongue.

Esti Hirlap reports on cultural events and general education and gives full details of forthcoming cultural activities. Colourful popularizing articles arouse interest and it often publishes interviews on various aspects of cultural life.

International cultural relations

Recognizing that international cultural co-operation can contribute to the spreading of understanding among peoples and to the establishment of a permanent basis for peaceful coexistence between countries having different social systems, the Hungarian People's Republic endeavours to develop cultural contacts with all countries.

A logical consequence of her peaceful foreign policy, this endeavour is reinforced by the fact that, as a country rather isolated by her language, Hungary is particularly concerned with cultural and artistic exchanges between States, and has accordingly developed widespread cultural contacts. There are inter-State and inter-institution scientific and cultural agreements on regular and many-sided co-operation with forty-six countries, and every effort is made to popularize foreign achievements in Hungary and Hungarian achievements abroad (15–18 per cent of the books annually published in Hungary are translations: over the past ten years 1,811 Russian, 918 French, 448 Czechoslovak, 1,046 German (including the German Democratic Republic, the Federal Republic of Germany and Austria) and 558 English). Over 5 million books were imported and 8.7 million exported in 1972; 160 foreign films were bought (including: Czechoslovakia, 11; France, 9; German Democratic Republic, 14; Italy, 13; Poland, 9; U.S.S.R., 36; United Kingdom, 10; United States, 26) and 94 Hungarian films were sold to 45 countries; 762,000 Hungarian records were exported and 386,000 imported.

Hungarian scientific and cultural organizations and cultural policy are involved in the work of over one hundred international organizations. Many of these organizations have held meetings in Hungary, for example, the International Federation of Library Associations, Jeunesses Musicales, International PEN. Every third or fourth year Budapest is the meeting-place of the poets of Europe; it is also the site of International Biennales of Small Sculpture.

Cultural and scientific agreements are of outstanding importance in

68

our international cultural relations. These agreements were started after the Second World War—mainly between socialist States because, in a socialist State, culture, education, science and development of research are considered State tasks, as schooling only used to be considered earlier.

The general pattern of cultural agreements is as follows. The framework of co-operation is established for a given period of time (e.g. five years). Representatives of the countries parties to the agreement—non-governmental delegations in most cases, often the leaders of institutions—meet to discuss working programmes for one or two years. Specialized institutions (e.g. associations of artists, the radio and television companies) often conclude direct contracts with their counterparts in the other country.

The main provisions are usually as follows: the parties may establish institutions in the other country with due regard to the laws in force there; they encourage cultural and artistic exchanges (journalists, ensembles, etc.); promote the exchange of literary and other works, publications, films, records for a better understanding of each other's country and culture. The experience gained in implementing cultural agreements is in general favourable. Co-operation is better planned, more conscious and wider than is possible through *ad hoc* contacts. The desire for planned contacts is increasing as international cultural relations develop. Hungary made cultural agreements, in the first place, with the friendly socialist countries, and now also has agreements with a number of developing countries and several capitalist States.

Co-operation is particularly intensive with the Soviet Union and the other friendly socialist countries. It evolved on the basis of identical ideologies and on the substantially identical practice of building socialism; it is deep-rooted and embraces all branches of cultural and artistic life. It is fundamentally based on a bilateral cultural agreement covering a long period within which the actual content is specified in working programmes valid for two to five years. The partner institutions sharing co-operation (e.g. ministries, artistic associations, book publishers, periodicals) also sign contracts or working programmes for one or two years. These contribute to the planned character and efficiency of the relations.

In the course of cultural and artistic exchanges the parties acquaint their people with the other country's outstanding classical literary and artistic creations (their 'golden treasury' of literature, for instance); there is a gradual exchange of contemporary arts (during the Festival of Hungarian Drama organized in the Soviet Union in 1971, for example, seventy-two Soviet theatres showed twenty-four Hungarian plays); a large number of films are regularly shown in each other's country; theatre companies and actors are sent and invited for guest performances; exhibitions display contemporary fine art; an extensive exchange of museum items is organized. (In 1970–71, for instance, a joint exhibition of the best classical items from the museums of fine arts of Budapest, Dresden, Leningrad and Prague was organized and has since been shown in all the co-operating countries.)

Various forms of co-operation have evolved in cultural relations with the other socialist countries: with several countries an intergovernmental or inter-ministerial mixed committee is responsible for co-ordinating co-operation; Hungarian book publishers have signed bilateral agreements with Soviet, Slovak, Yugoslav and Romanian publishers on the joint publishing of books in Hungarian; the artistic associations and cultural periodicals organize common cultural and art conferences. Another important feature of the relations is their dynamic growth.

The agreements concluded with countries that have recently acquired independence have a specific importance. In keeping with her policy of using cultural means to aid developing countries politically, economically and in all other ways, Hungary endeavours to promote the formation of the national intelligentsia and the prosperity of the national culture.

These are the principles and considerations that underlie agreements concluded with Algeria, Dahomey, Egypt, Ethiopia, Ghana, Guinea, India, Iraq, Kuwait, Mali, Tanzania and Yemen. Much attention is devoted to possibilities of taking part in each other's university training through scholarships (which are also awarded to students studying on their own). In most of these agreements the parties undertake to give a clear and true picture of the other country in their textbooks on history and geography. They encourage the translation of important works issued in the other party's country, the exchange of books, periodicals, publications and antiquities. The agreements also stipulate arrangements for reciprocal visits by delegations.

The Hungarian organizations engaged in fostering international cultural relations—in the spirit of the peaceful foreign policy of the Hungarian People's Republic and in compliance with the principles of peaceful coexistence of countries having different social systems—strive to develop cultural relations also with capitalist countries. They are guided by the consideration that co-operation should involve the exchange of real cultural, artistic values and must not allow a decisive influence to private business considerations that—as experience shows—occasionally hamper such international exchanges.

Among the capitalist countries with which Hungary has co-operation agreements are Belgium, Finland, France and Italy. The traditionally extensive Finno-Hungarian contacts are closely related to Finno-Ugric kinship. Hungarian-French and Hungarian-Italian cultural relations also have a long traditional history.

The international cultural relations of Hungary are co-ordinated by the Institute for Cultural Relations. The Ministry of Culture is intensively concerned with these relations and has a separate department for them. The Hungarian National Commission for Unesco and Hungarian artistic associations are also closely involved. The distribution of Hungarian books, records, periodicals and so on is the responsibility of the foreign trade enterprise 'Kultura'. A Hungarian Cultural Institute operates in such capital cities as Berlin, Sofia and Warsaw. Prague has a Hungarian cultural centre. The Hungarian Academy in Rome, the Hungarian Institute in Paris and the Collegium Hungaricum in Vienna have also existed for several decades.

Appendix   Statistical tables

TABLE 1   Some characteristic features

Per 100 inhabitants	1950	1960	1970	1972
Number of copies of newspapers	12[1]	14	21	24
Copies of books and booklets	649	417	559	677
Number of volumes lent from public libraries	180[2]	300	530	560
Radio licences	7	22	25	25
Television licences	—	1	17	20
Visits to theatres	32	64	54	54
Visits to concerts	4	13	14	17
Attendance at educational lectures	...	69	45	42
Attendance at recitals	...	108[3]	66	66
Visits to museums	14	36	69	76
Visits to cinemas	500	1,400	800	700

1. 1952.
2. 1953.
3. 1962.
— Nil or negligible.
... Data not available.

TABLE 2   Book publishing

	1938	1950	1960	1970	1972
Number of titles of books and booklets published	5,611	4,219	5,335	5,238	7,293
(of which: literature and juvenile books)	(1,231)	(541)	(949)	(916)	(993)
Number of copies published (in millions)	16.8	60.6	41.6	57.8	70.0
(of which: literature and juvenile books)	(6.9)	(4.6)	(15.4)	(15.8)	(21.7)
Average number of copies per title	2,992	14,367	7,807	11,033	9,605
(of which: literature and juvenile books)	(5,581)	(8,559)	(16,187)	(17,216)	(21,811)

TABLE 3   Publication of literature

	1950	1960	1970	1972
Number of titles of books and booklets published	438	711	673	739
(of which:				
works by Hungarian authors	(...)	(354)	(353)	(388)
works by foreign authors)	(...)	(357)	(320)	(351)
Number of copies published (in millions)	3.5	10.4	10.9	14.7
(of which:				
works by Hungarian authors	(...)	(4.8)	(4.8)	(6.5)
works by foreign authors)	(...)	(5.6)	(6.1)	(8.2)
Average number of copies per title	8,043	14,616	16,207	19,886
(of which:				
works by Hungarian authors	(...)	(12,240)	(13,532)	(16,779)
works by foreign authors	(...)	(15,537)	(19,157)	(23,319)

TABLE 4   Publication of newspapers and periodicals

	1950	1960	1970	1972
Number of titles of newspapers and periodicals	334	590	859	867
(of which dailies)	(24)	(24)	(29)	(29)
Number of copies of newspapers and periodicals (in millions)	474.5	704.6	1,101.0	1,131.0
(of which dailies)	(290.8)	(472.3)	(730.8)	(750.0)
Average number of copies per periodical (in thousands)	1,421	1,194	1,282	1,304

TABLE 5   Public libraries

	1950	1960	1970	1971	1972
Number of libraries	4,333	9,773	9,251	8,845	8,720
Stock of books (in million volumes)	2.2	11.1	24.7	27.0	26.0
Number of registered borrowers (in thousands)	402.6	1,627.0	2,224.7	2,231.0	2,253.3
Number of volumes loaned out to users (in millions)	6.2	30.2	54.8	55.9	57.7
Stock of books per inhabitant	0.2	1.1	2.4	2.5	2.6
Number of volumes loaned out per registered borrower	15	19	25	25	26

TABLE 6 Theatres

	1950	1960	1970	1972
Number of theatres	17	32	34	34
Number of performances	6,604	12,702	11,991	12,022
(of which in rural communities)	(848)	(2,989)	(2,713)	(2,225)
Annual attendance (in thousands)	2,961	6,429	5,591	5,616
(of which in rural communities)	(239)	(782)	(790)	(627)

TABLE 7 Number of theatre performances and attendance according to types of performance

	1955	1960	1970	1972
Number of performances				
Plays in prose	6,390	6,192	5,302	6,113
Musical plays	3,182	4,045	3,316	2,548
Operas, ballets	814	894	779	933
Puppet shows or plays	697	1,019	1,563	1,337
Literary programmes	—	150	194	313
Mixed, variety shows and juvenile pieces	619	402	837	778
TOTAL	11,702	12,702	11,991	12,022
Annual attendance (in thousands)				
Plays in prose	3,087.5	2,797.6	2,479.8	2,648.1
Musical plays	1,870.3	1,894.6	1,473.9	1,311.0
Operas, ballets	1,327.5	1,215.3	785.0	851.4
Puppet shows or plays	189.1	315.1	471.2	406.3
Literary programmes	—	46.6	52.2	67.6
Mixed, variety shows and juvenile pieces	273.2	160.2	329.2	331.8
TOTAL	6,747.6	6,429.4	5,591.3	5,612.2

TABLE 8 Concerts

	1950	1960	1970	1972
Number of concerts (serious music, light music and estrade)	507	2,420	3,251	3,774
Audience (in thousands)	380.0	1,322.0	1,495.0	1,739.5

77

TABLE 9   Cinemas

	1935	1950	1960	1970	1972
Number of fixed cinemas	599	1,549	4,558	3,879	3,756
(of which in rural communities)	...	(686)	(3,716)	(3,306)	(3,177)
Number of cinemas suitable for projecting wide-screen pictures	—	—	158	2,605	2,713
Number of performances (in thousands)	148.9	294.5	845.7	753.8	722.4
(of which in rural communities)	(...)	(141.4)	(554.7)	(492.5)	(458.7)
Annual attendance (in millions)	18.5	47.1	140.1	79.6	74.4
(of which in rural communities)	(...)	(16.4)	(62.3)	(30.9)	(27.9)
Number of feature films shown	224	59	148	167	164
(of which Hungarian productions)	(14)	(4)	(17)	(24)	(23)

TABLE 10   Radio

	1938	1950	1960	1970	1972
Number of licences (in thousands)	419.2	619.5	2,223.7	2,530.3	2,542.2
(of which in rural communities)	(...)	(162.5)	(1,031.0)	(1,210.7)	(1,187.3)
Number of licences per 1,000 inhabitants	46	66	222	245	245
(of which in rural communities)	(...)	(28)	(173)	(222)	(220)

TABLE 11   Television

	1958	1960	1970	1972
Number of licences (in thousands)	16.0	103.7	1,768.6	2,084.7
(of which in rural communities)	(1.9)	(19.2)	(770.2)	(942.0)
Number of licences per 1,000 inhabitants	2.0	10	171	201
(of which in rural communities)	(0.3)	(3)	(142)	(175)

TABLE 12   Duration of broadcasting (weekly average in hours)

Service	1950	1960	1970	1972
Radio	222	227	265	328
Television	—	22	51	55

TABLE 13   Mass cultural movement

	1953	1960	1970[1]	1972
Number of cultural halls	2,265	2,770	3,656	2,825
Educational lectures:				
Number	181,664	118,645	109,159	100,557
Attendance (in millions)	10.7	6.9	4.7	4.4
Number of professional circles	3,673	6,102	5,787	6,252
Number of amateur art groups	18,046	12,162	9,645	9,181
Evenings with entertainment programmes:				
Number	63,203	47,793	31,025	32,096
Attendance (in millions)	. . .	10.3	6.8	6.9

1. *Hungarian Statistical Yearbook, 1971.*

TABLE 14   Museums

	1935	1950	1960	1970	1972
Number of museums	46	62	93	183	189
Number of exhibitions	. . .	. . .	809	1,432	1,406
Number of visitors (in thousands)	791.6	1,307.5	3,640.3	7,153.5	7,881.3